Contractor Stories

Contractor Stories

Inspirational Lessons for Contractors with a Burning Desire to Succeed!

Matt Michel

Coldstream Press

Copyright © 2023 by Matt Michel.

All characters appearing in this work are fictitious. Any resemblance to real persons, living or dead, is purely coincidental.

All rights reserved. Designed and printed in the United States of America. No part of this book may be used or reproduced in any manner whatsoever without written permission except in the case of brief quotations embodied in critical articles and reviews. For information, contact:

Coldstream Press
601 Paradise Cove
Denton, TX 76208

ISBN: 979-8-218-41817-5

Contact the author at MattMichel@Mail.com

Designed and printed in the USA

Jesu Juva

Contents

Foreword 1

The Story Behind Contractor Stories 3

1. The Coffee Conversation 5

2. A Can of Success 11

3. The Decision 21

4. Why 33

5. The Start of Plumbing Season 45

6. Everybody Sells 51

7. Fear 65

8. Marketing 77

9. Slump 91

10. Family Business 101

About Matt Michel 118

Foreword by Mark Matteson

I met Matt Michel in 2002 at a Comfortech gathering. He had just launched the Service Roundtable and it only took me about five minutes to realize he was the smartest guy in the room. With a Chesire Cat grin he asks the hard questions and uses the Socratic method to challenge your assumptions about the industry and change the way we see the world of service businesses.

Matt is a gifted raconteur, a teller of tales, a superlative sage who knows the service industry and construction trades from top to bottom. I convinced him to join me in 2009 at a construction conference in Istanbul, Turkey. He quite simply stole the show, sharing his insights on commodity branding. That's the thing about Matt: He can and does talk about every facet of business, from marketing, branding, sales, and hiring to alliances, social media, tech sales, performance, and profit. He's a polyglot of sorts, someone who speaks many languages. Matt speaks the language of every facet of his business. He is a sponge.

A voracious reader, he blends his writing voice with his speaking voice in a unique and authentic way. *Contractor Stories* is a bit like cheesecake. Take it one bite at a time, but don't let the short chapters fool you. Each one covers a different topic and ends with a simple yet powerful summary of takeaways that will change your business and your life. I read it in one sitting. I could not put it down! I said "YES!" on every page.

This is the kind of book you buy for every employee and make it mandatory reading. The characters he has created pull you into the stories, yet you will find yourself taking notes and capturing ideas to improve profit, productivity, and morale in your business. It is, quite simply, a master class in leadership.

Having shared many a stage around the world with Matt over the last 21 years, I can tell you from personal experience that he's still the smartest guy in the room. More than that, he's a loving husband and a great father to his two daughters. I would trust him with my checkbook and my children; you can trust that his new book will change your life. I know it changed mine. I am making it the book of the month for my newsletter and I can't wait to have him as a guest on my podcast to promote this amazing series of stories.

The subtitle of *Contractor Stories* could be *Tips and Tales from My Travels* because that's what he has captured and shared. Gathering up a lifetime of helping contractors succeed, he has assembled a series of stories you won't want to miss. Thank you, Matt. As Steve Jobs said, "We're here to make a dent in the universe." Thank you for letting me ride shotgun.

Mark Matteson
Bestselling Author, International Speaker

The Story Behind *Contractor Stories*

I was sitting in an airport bar with Dan, an advertising agency account executive. He described how a company I worked for regarded contractors. He said, "There's a sense of reverence for them. They're on a pedestal."

Dan was right. That was exactly how we looked at the contractors who bought and installed the products we manufactured. Through the years and decades, I've never lost that sense of reverence for contractors and I still put them on a pedestal. After all, they are the people who keep the lights on at night. They keep our carpets clean. They keep our homes cool in the summer and warm in the winter. They keep the rain out. They make sure our toilets flush. They keep our showers hot. They keep our homes free of insects and pests. They keep our appliances working. They repair the damage we cause and make the improvements we envision. When our homes get outdated, they update them.

We couldn't function as a society without the contractors who make our homes livable and comfortable. They deserve lives of prosperity for providing services we cannot live without, yet too many of them barely get by. They may have gone to trade school and learned how to turn a wrench, but no one taught them how to turn a profit.

I've spent most of my life working in contracting or in support of contractors, playing my part to help them achieve greater levels of performance and profitability than many imagined was possible.

Contractor Stories

For my efforts, one national trade magazine called me "The Contractors' Advocate." Another called me their "North Star." Even though I've stepped down from my role running the world's largest contractor business alliance, I still want to serve contractors through writing and speaking. This book is one step along the way.

Contractor Stories is not your typical business book. It's a series of short stories featuring contractors, each one with a lesson or two. Each story reflects the real-world fears, doubts, and triumphs that contractors experience. Each story is relatable.

Why stories? Stories are in our DNA. Long before we had a written language, we sat around campfires while the tribal elders told stories that people needed to hear in order to survive. Where do we find food? How do we avoid danger?

We learn by listening to stories. We pay attention to them. We remember them. There's a reason Christ used parables to teach lessons. Over two thousand years later we still study them.

I've found that stories also resonate with contractors. The people who gravitate towards contracting tend to be a little ADHD. I know because I am the same. Consuming non-fiction is a chore at best, so I wrote *Contractor Stories* as a series of short, fictional stories that are easy to read and remember. Read this book, one story at a time, in any order you want. If you find it helpful, pass it along or recommend it to another contractor. All of them—and you—deserve lives of prosperity.

Matt Michel
Speaker/Writer/Rancher
Ranchlands of Texas, LLC

1

The Coffee Conversation

Jerry sat in the coffee shop, sipping on an overpriced cup of Sumatra, and stared at his phone. The coffee was a small luxury he should have passed on, but he craved caffeine. He tried to enjoy it. There didn't seem to be much he could enjoy lately. Little did he know that the older gentleman who asked if he could share his table in the crowded coffee shop would change his worldview.

"Excuse me," Jerry heard. "Do you mind if I share your table?"

Jerry looked up. The man was cheerful and elderly with a head full of grey hair. Jerry said, "Sure, take a chair."

"I just don't get it," Jerry mumbled to himself.

"Get what?" the man asked.

Jerry sighed. In a rush, he said, "I don't get anything. I don't understand the world. I don't know why everything costs so much, why I can't get air handlers for my business, why I can't find employees, why the economy is tanking, anything."

Contractor Stories

The old man said, "Yes, that's a lot. What do you do?"

"I'm a plumbing and air conditioning contractor."

"I thought contractors had been doing pretty well," the old man countered.

"Well, yeah, but that's not the future. I mean, things don't look good."

The old man took a sip of his coffee. He said, "Do you mean things don't look good in general or things don't look good for you in particular?"

Jerry wondered why the heck he was talking to this man, but it felt good to unload a little. He answered, "For... well, everything. I feel like nothing is in my control."

"But you own a company?"

"Yeah. So?"

"Don't you control your company?"

"Somewhat," said Jerry. "It's so hard to find people, so my employees know they have me over a barrel. If I ask them to do something they don't want to do, they quit."

"You mean you have to persuade them and lead them instead of simply ordering them? And that you control how you address them and lead them?"

"Uh, well, when you put it like that it sounds different."

"I think you have more control than you think."

"What do you know about it?" barked Jerry. He was getting tired of the old man.

"Whoa. I'm not trying to argue with you or interrupt your pity party. I'm just trying to have a conversation over a cup of coffee. I can leave if you'd like."

"No," said Jerry. "Sorry. I'm just frustrated."

"Well, I can understand that. But you said you can't control anything. Are you sure?"

"What do you mean?"

"You can control your attitude, right? I mean, you may not be able to control what happens to you, but you can control how you respond, right?"

"I suppose."

"You're the leader of your company. It's my experience that the people in an organization respond to and reflect their leaders, but they also amplify them. If you look scared, they think the worst, expect their jobs are in jeopardy, and start looking for new ones. It works the same way in reverse. If you're confident and positive, they will be too. Does that make sense?"

"Uh, a little," said Jerry.

"Then you also seem worried about business."

"I am."

"But people can't live without plumbing, heating, and air conditioning, right?"

"Yeah, but we're still getting fewer calls," said Jerry.

"So, what can you do about it?"

"I don't know."

"What are your competitors doing?"

"Most of them are like me. They don't know what to do, but they worry about money so they cut spending as much as they can."

"Why?"

"Why? So they don't run out of money," said Jerry.

"So," said the old man, "they are worried about money because there are fewer calls, which means it's harder to find customers, so they cut back on their efforts to find them? That doesn't make sense."

"Not when you put it like that."

"But you don't have to be like them, do you? I mean, you control your marketing, advertising, and sales, right?"

"Uh, well. Yeah. I guess."

"Do you or don't you?"

"I do," said Jerry forcefully.

Contractor Stories

"So, what do you think will happen if you put forth more effort to get customers when your competitors are doing less?"

"I'll get more customers? And... and I'll get customers *they* might get under other circumstances?"

"Kinda what I think."

Jerry thought for a second. It made sense. He said, "So you're saying I can't control prices, inflation, or the economy, but I can control my attitude and I can control how my company responds."

"Exactly, except you *can* control your prices."

"To a limit."

"Really? You just paid six dollars for a buck's worth of coffee."

"Well, I really needed some caffeine."

"And you don't think people really need plumbing? Or heating? Or air conditioning?"

Jerry looked the man up and down. "Who are you?"

The old man smiled. "I'm someone who was just like you. I used to own a contracting company and sold it years ago for a few million. I saw you get out of your truck and thought I'd strike up a conversation."

"Why?"

"When I was coming up in the business and struggling, older contractors helped me. For the longest time I didn't trust them. Then I realized they were simply paying forward the help they received. This is a great business, a great industry. You have more control over your life and business than almost any of the people you see working in the high-rise corporate cube farms that surround this coffee shop. If there's a recession, you can decide whether you want to participate in it or not. Personally, I would advise against participating. I never did."

"Thank you," said Jerry.

The old man—the old contractor—shrugged, got up, and said on the way out, "Thank me by paying it forward."

Jerry looked at his coffee. Yeah, he could probably charge more. If he did, he could market more. He took a sip and relished the taste. He realized it was up to him whether he enjoyed things or not. Like the old contractor said, he had more control than he thought.

Jerry got out his phone, opened a notes app, and typed some notes from his coffee conversation.

Notes from the Coffee Conversation

- I control my attitude.

- I control how I respond to circumstances.

- I control how I lead my team.

- I control the example I set.

- I control my pricing.

- I control my marketing.

- I decide whether or not to participate in a recession.

2

A Can of Success

Tommy was having a bad day. It started at breakfast. The IKEA chair he assembled the night before collapsed when he sat on it and everything had been downhill from there. What he didn't know was that fate was about to intervene.

When he got to work, his boss called him into his office. "Son," he said, "I'm sorry, but corporate asked me to make a headcount reduction. You're the last person hired so, unfortunately, you're also the first to be laid off."

Just like that, Tommy was jobless. Could this day get any worse, he thought? Then his phone rang.

Tommy smiled when he looked at the caller ID. It was his girlfriend. "Hi, babe," he answered.

"Tommy," she said. "We've got to talk."

Uh oh. He pulled over and turned off the car. "Why? What's up?"

"We need to talk in person."

"What's wrong with now?"

She sighed. "If you insist. I got offered a job today. I'm going to take it."

"Hey, that's great."

"The job is based in New York. I'm moving in two weeks."

"New York? I can't move to New York."

"I know, Tommy. I don't expect you to follow me to New York, but I really want this job. So I guess this is goodbye."

"Is that it?"

"I'm sorry, Tommy. I told you this was a possibility. Look, I'm getting a call from my new boss. I have to go."

She hung up and Tommy just sat there. If he was honest, he knew they hadn't had the greatest relationship and she probably wasn't the right person for him, but he felt she was the best he could do. *I can't believe this,* he thought. Fired from a crummy job and dumped by a crummy girlfriend on the same crummy day. What else could go wrong to make the crummy day even crummier?

When Tommy started his car, he heard a clicking sound, then nothing. *Freaking great. Just freaking great!*

Tommy got out and kicked the tire. Hard. "Ow," he screamed. "Crap that hurt."

Tommy felt his heart racing. He needed to calm down and cool off. It was hot and humid outside, so he stepped into the store next to where he was parked. Stenciled on the door was *The Fate Store.*

As he walked in, a bell chimed. "Welcome to The Fate Store," proclaimed a short, bald, Asian man. "Have you come to choose a new fate for yourself?"

"Huh," said Tommy. "*What* are you selling?"

"I sell fate. Fate brought you here so you must need to change your fate. Come, come. You see the cans of fate. Find your fate."

Tommy looked around and saw stacks and stacks of small cans, each one neatly labeled. He grabbed one at random. "A LIFE OF MISERY," read Tommy. "Who would want a life of misery?"

"You'd be surprised," said the proprietor. "Many people choose misery. Why? I don't know. I don't know. People decide they want failed marriages. Why? I don't know. I don't know."

Tommy examined more cans. He discarded *A LIFE SPENT LIVING IN THE PAST*, *A LIFE OBSESSED WITH WHAT COULD HAVE BEEN*, and *A LIFE OF MISTAKE AFTER MISTAKE*.

"Uh, sorry," Tommy remarked, "but these suck."

"Ah," said the proprietor, "Many fates 'suck' as you say, but they are very, very popular. People select them when they could choose other fates. Why? I don't know. I don't know."

"YAW!" screamed Tommy, dropping *A LIFE OF MISFORTUNE*. "I've had enough of this."

"Then keep looking," encouraged the proprietor. "Keep looking. Your fate is here. You merely need to choose it."

"Hey, look at this one," said Tommy. It was labeled *A SUCCESSFUL LIFE*. "This is more like it. How much does this cost?"

"Ah. What is the price of success, of a successful life? It is something that you pay for over time. A lot of success costs more than a little success."

"I don't know," said Tommy. "I don't have much money now."

"No money down. You can sign," said the proprietor. "Here, here. Sign this." He pulled a piece of paper from a drawer.

Tommy read it. The headline was *Bill of Sale*. It read simply, *I, the undersigned, do hereby commit to paying the price of a successful life in accordance with the success I achieve.*

"It still doesn't say how much. I don't like committing to an open-ended charge."

"Ah," said the proprietor. "That is because the payment is entirely up to you. You decide how much to pay, when to pay, where to pay, and how to pay. Just sign."

"Okay. How do I pay? Do I come here?"

"The universe will collect. Fate will collect," said the proprietor.

Oh, what the heck, thought Tommy. He signed.

"Congratulations," said the proprietor. "You have started your journey."

"Yeah, now if I could only start my car."

"What does the can say?" asked the proprietor.

Tommy looked. "It says, 'Shake whenever you need more success. Open when you no longer need more success.'"

"So shake," said the proprietor.

Tommy felt foolish, but he shook the can anyway. He wasn't sure, but he thought he heard something rattling around in the can.

"Let's look at your car and see if you can start it," suggested the proprietor.

Tommy walked out with the proprietor and popped the hood at the proprietor's request. He tried to start the car, but after the click, click, click, he stopped. The proprietor reached into his back pocket, removed a huge wrench, and hammered it against the starter. "Try it now," he suggested.

The car turned right over. "Hey, thanks," said Tommy. When he jumped out to close the hood the proprietor was nowhere to be seen. The door to the store was locked.

Whatever, Tommy thought. *Now I just need a job where I can be successful.* He thought for a moment. *Why not?* Again, feeling a little foolish, he shook the can of success and pulled out into traffic. Immediately in front of him was a high cube van with a large sign on the back: *Now hiring. No experience necessary. Will train.*

Tommy thought this must be some kind of a sign. He followed the truck into a fenced yard next to a building with an identical sign on it. The company name was SmithCo. Tommy got out, walked in, applied for the job, was interviewed on the spot by Dan Smith, the owner, and was hired. Even better, SmithCo paid more than the warehouse job he just lost. Tommy had never been so successful when looking for a job.

Over the next week, Tommy was offered basic training by SmithCo's service manager and was given a variety of tasks around the shop, such as cleaning, counting inventory, and so on. He was given books to take home and study to speed along his progress. Every morning the service manager quizzed him about what he learned the day before.

When he was satisfied with his basic knowledge, the service manager assigned Tommy to work as an apprentice for Stanley, one of the senior technicians. "Pay attention," urged the service manager, "because you can learn a lot from Stanley."

On the morning he was to start riding with Stanley, Tommy shook the can of success like crazy. Stanley greeted him at the shop door. Tommy took to him immediately and Stanley seemed grateful for someone to help him with the physical work.

"Kid, this is a good company and a great industry," Stanley said. "Once you learn the trade, you'll never lack work. Even if you do something else, you can always fall back on the trade. Plus, there are no limits on how successful you can become. If you want to start your own company someday, you can probably do it."

"Excuse me for asking, but how come you haven't started your own company?"

Stanley laughed. "Kid, I did. I did okay for a few years, but I just wasn't willing to pay the price to be a successful business owner. I didn't like marketing. I hated the government paperwork. I just like fixing stuff. One day, Danny Smith asked me if I wouldn't rather sell to him and go to work for him. He said I'd make more money and have fewer headaches. And he was right. I'm happy doing what I like, which is fixing stuff."

Hmm, thought Tommy. *Pay the price. Well, I'm willing to pay the price. Maybe I can run my own company one day.*

As the weeks passed, and Tommy learned the trade from Stanley, he felt more confident about everything else in his life, especially when he shook the can of success. He shook it before rebuilding the IKEA chair and it held together. He even shook it when a blonde moved into his apartment complex.

Tommy was hardly a ladies' man. Asking her out was outkicking his coverage, but after shaking the can of success he felt emboldened to try. His usual lame approach was to look at his shoes and say something like, *You wouldn't want to go out with me, would you?* Instead, when he ran into the blonde at the apartment complex's mailboxes, he asked, "Hey, you're new here, right?"

"I am," she said.

He extended his hand. "Tommy."

She took it. "Beth."

"Pleasure to meet you, Beth. Where are you from?"

"New York," Beth answered.

Tommy nearly choked: His ex was in New York by now. "New York? Wow. It's got to be an adjustment moving here."

Beth laughed. "Yeah, it is. There are more good changes than bad changes."

"What are good changes?"

"I really like the outdoors, the fresh air. Despite living in the city, I've never been much of a city girl."

Tommy jumped in. "So why don't I show you one of the greatest trails in the area? Don't worry, it's well-traveled, and the waterfall at the end is amazing."

Beth pondered a moment. "Sounds terrific," she said.

Go for it, Tommy thought. "How about Saturday? We could hike the trail and have a picnic lunch at the waterfall."

"Deal," said Beth. "But I get to pack the lunch."

When Tommy got back to his apartment, he literally kissed the can of success. "You," he said to the can, "are amazing."

***

Fast forward 30 years. Tommy is cutting his grass and looking at his mobile phone after every pass, watching his bank account. He had just sold his business for a 10X multiple on three million dollars of EBITDA and was waiting for the money to hit. Finally, the number changed: *a 30-million-dollar deposit!*

"Yes!" he screamed to no one. He rushed into the house and held out his phone. "Beth, look at this!"

"I can't even wrap my head around this," she said, "but I knew you would be a success from the moment we met."

Beth hugged and kissed her husband. When they broke, Tommy went to his home office. He opened a drawer and pulled out the can of success. He read the label. *Open when you no longer need more success.*

Tommy reflected. He'd had a great life. It all started when he walked into The Fate Store, which he could never find later. He'd searched for it many times but never could locate the street. Whenever he asked people about The Fate Store no one had ever heard of it or its funny little proprietor.

At SmithCo he put in the effort as an apprentice and earned his own truck. While he never started his own company, he did advance to service manager. Later, he bought SmithCo from Dan Smith, who, along with Stanley, had become one of his mentors.

Over the last few years it was Tommy's turn to serve as a mentor to others. Some were employees. Others were contractors he met in business alliance meetings. One was even a local competitor. So much had been given to him that Tommy felt called, compelled even, to give back to others. It seemed that whatever he gave he received back just as much, if not more.

Under Tommy's leadership, SmithCo grew and became more profitable. He rarely shook the can of success anymore, yet success still seemed to follow him.

Not only was his professional life blessed, but his personal life also exceeded every expectation. He was married to the woman of

Contractor Stories

his dreams and had awesome kids, which he credited to Beth more than to his efforts. While he managed to attend the school plays and afternoon sporting events, Beth played a greater part in raising their kids than he could. It was part of the price he paid for growing a successful company.

Tommy rotated the can and read the label again. *Shake whenever you need to have more success. Open when you no longer need more success.*

He rocked back in his chair and thought about the success he'd enjoyed. It was time. He walked to the kitchen, grabbed a can opener, and opened the can.

Inside were several numbered pieces of cardboard with writing on them. He read the first one: *Success does not come from a can.*

The second one said, *Success comes from hard work, the belief that you can succeed, and the willingness to take risks and venture forth.*

On the last was written, *If this can helped you achieve a successful life, it was only because it helped you gain the confidence needed to believe you could succeed, to take the risks necessary to succeed, and to venture forth. The hard work was all yours. All you needed was confidence.*

Tommy leaned back and smiled. *Yeah,* he thought. Before he walked into The Fate Store he lacked confidence in himself. Because of that he didn't think he could succeed and wasn't willing to risk the effort success required. The can of success was nothing more than a ploy to get him to believe in himself, but it was a ploy that changed the trajectory of this life.

On the final piece of cardboard Tommy read, *Success is a journey, not a destination. The successful life is one well-lived.*

Indeed, he thought.

Success does not come from a can.

Success comes from hard work,
the belief you can succeed,
and the willingness to take risks
and venture forth.

Success is a journey, not a destination.
The successful life is one well-lived.

3

The Decision

Jim was feeling the pressure. He was getting it from his friends. He was getting it from his parents. He was getting it from his teachers. Everyone wanted to know about his college plans. Jim's problem? He didn't want to go anywhere.

What *would* he do? He was a decent student. He did well on his SATs and he always figured he would go to college like everyone else. But lately he was having second thoughts.

First, Jim overheard his sister and brother-in-law talking. He'd gone to their apartment to swim in the pool. After he was done and toweling off, he went to their apartment to say goodbye and overheard a pretty intense discussion in the kitchen.

"Kim, we just can't afford it," said Frank. "We can't even afford a decent place to live."

"But the government keeps pausing the loan repayment and there's talk of the loan forgiveness."

"Nothing's been forgiven yet," said Frank. "I don't think we can hope for that. I mean, we do owe the money."

"It's just so unfair. I mean, that's not how it's supposed to work. We'll never be able to pay our college loans back."

"Now Kim. Don't say never. It's just going to take time."

"Take time? We're going to spend a decade or more paying back loans from four years of college. At this rate, we won't be able to afford to start a family until we're in our thirties."

Jim heard his sister softly crying and quietly slipped out without interrupting. What he heard was a shock. He knew college was expensive, but wow. And he knew his parents would help as much as they could, but they didn't have that much money and Jim had two younger brothers.

If he went to college, he would have to take out his own set of loans. One of Jim's better traits was his frugality. He didn't want to go into debt, especially not big-time debt.

While the conversation he overheard was giving him second thoughts, one of his best friends gave him more to think about. Dale had already applied to Tech and been accepted. He wanted Jim to attend with him.

"C'mon Jim," urged Dale. "Get off your butt and get your application in. It'll be great. We can room together and pledge my big brother's fraternity."

"I don't know, man. I don't even know what I want to major in."

"It doesn't matter. The classes are all bull anyway unless you want to major in engineering," said Dale, making a retching sound. "My brother says the profs let you know what they want to hear and you just repeat it back for the grade."

"What do you mean?"

"Except for the engineering professors and a few of the business professors, all they want is for you to give them some politically correct, woke crap on tests and you'll ace everything.

It's just like Mrs. Warren's government class. Argue and she beats you down. Agree and she passes you."

"So what's the point of going to college?" asked Jim.

"Par-tayyys," replied Dale. "Mixers with sororities. Four freaking years of sowing our oats. It'll be awesome."

Jim just shook his head. It wasn't that he didn't like fun. He did. But shouldn't he learn something? The only thing he learned from Mrs. Warren was that he hated politics. If that was the norm in college, why should he go into debt for four years of political indoctrination? Did he have to go into debt to meet girls? Well, maybe that was a dumb question. Did he have to go into a decade's worth of debt?

His problem was he didn't know what he wanted to do if he didn't go to school. He had considered the military. When he talked with Mr. Simpson, who lived next door, that idea died.

"Look, Jim," Mr. Simpson explained. "I'm the last guy to tell someone not to go into the military. It made me who I am. I mean, I flew fu..., uh, I flew freaking jets off aircraft carriers. Do you want to know one of the scariest things in the world?"

"Yeah, I know," said Jim. "It's landing on an aircraft carrier at night in a storm."

"Hmm. Guess I've told you about that."

"Yeah," said Jim. "And I get it. But I don't have to fly jets. I might go into the Marines."

"Do you know why the Navy allows marines on ships?" asked Mr. Simpson.

"Yeah, I know. So the sailors will have someone to dance with."

"Guess I've told you that one, too."

"Maybe once or twice," said Jim. "But I still think the Marines are badass."

"Let's hope they still are," said Mr. Simpson. "I don't know if you've been keeping track with what's going on in the service, but, and I say this with a little unease..."

"What?" demanded Jim.

"I'm worried about our fighting forces. The military seems more worried about politics than our ability to make war. I saw a Navy training video recently where the entirety of the video was about the proper use of pronouns. Training should be about defeating the enemy, not fu..., uh, *freaking* pronouns."

More politics, thought Jim. It was everywhere. "Okay, Mr. Simpson. I get you. I just have to figure something out."

Jim went home. At dinner, his parents asked him about his college applications. "I don't know if I want to go to college," he answered.

"What?" asked his dad. "You are going to go to college."

"Why?"

"Because that's how you get ahead in this life."

"You mean the way Kim and Frank are buried under their loans?" asked Jim.

"Hey," said his father.

"I don't want to be an engineer and I don't want to tell professors what they want to hear simply to get grades."

"Peace," interjected Jim's mom.

Needing to get in the last word, his dad added, "If you don't go to college, you can't expect to hang around here without paying your way. You need to get a job."

"Fine," said Jim.

"Fine," said his dad.

After dinner, Jim started scrolling through the job ads on his phone. The first looked promising, but then he realized it was selling overpriced cutlery. That sucked.

The next one was setting appointments for door-to-door vacuum cleaner sales. That sucked more.

Then he saw one that seemed appealing. It stated, *Are you mechanically inclined? Are you a people person? Are you also money-motivated? We'll pay you $2 per hour over minimum wage for a training wage. Attend our academy, get paid to learn, earn* more down the road, plus benefits. We offer careers in an essential industry that protects the health of the nation. Call King Plumbing at 555-1221 for more information.

Jim was familiar with John King, the Plumbing King. His ads were everywhere. But plumbing? He didn't want to be a plumber. How do you get girls when you're a plumber? He kept scrolling. But one after another, he either didn't qualify or the jobs sucked.

At school the next day, he kept thinking about the Plumbing King ad. It wouldn't hurt to find out a little more. After school, he called the number. "It's a great day at King Plumbing where we treat our customers like royalty. How can I serve you?" answered a cheerful female voice.

"Uh, hi," said Jim. "I'm calling about the ad for the academy."

"Oh, terrific," replied Miss Enthusiastic. "Let me connect you with our recruiter."

Jim heard the phone ring. "This is Stephanie. How can I serve you?"

"Uh, hi," said Jim. "My name is Jim Marshall and I'm sort of interested in the academy, but I'm still in school."

"No worries," said Stephanie. "We have another class starting mid-June. Will you be out by then?"

"I'd better be."

"Okay, so you are aware, we require a personality test and mechanical aptitude test before we accept you into the academy. Should you pass those, we will conduct background checks and administer a drug test. There won't be a problem, will there?"

"Uh, no ma'am. But, well, it's just that..."

"Yes?"

"Well, I don't know if I want to be a plumber. I don't know if that's right for me."

"I see," said Stephanie. "Can I put you on hold for a second?"

"Sure," said Jim. He wondered if he should just hang up. Maybe this wasn't a great idea.

"Mr. Marshall," said Stephanie, returning to the line. "Would you be able to drop by our office later this afternoon? Mr. King would like to meet you and talk with you about the plumbing profession to see if it's right for you."

"Mr. King? Like, the guy on the ads? John King the Plumbing King?"

Stephanie laughed a little. "One and the same. Would 4:00 or 4:30 be better for you?"

"I guess 4:00."

"Okay. Are you calling from your mobile?"

"Yeah."

"I'll text you the address."

Just like that Jim found himself with an appointment to meet a guy who was somewhat of a local celebrity.

***

At 4:00 Jim entered King Plumbing's offices. "You must be Mr. Marshall," said a peppy woman who sounded like the person on the phone. "Take a seat and I'll ring Stephanie."

Stephanie arrived and handed Jim a stack of forms. "This is a personality profile. Just answer it as honestly as you can. We use these to help ensure that we're putting people in the right seats. In other words, we know the type of personality types who do well in the different positions we offer. We won't try to put you into a job you won't like or succeed at. The next test is the mechanical aptitude test. It helps us assess whether you have the innate ability to do the work. Next is our application, which you will need to complete. Finally, here are some brochures on the academy and on the company."

"Wow," said Jim. He was a little overwhelmed. His stereotype of plumbers was that they were little more than knuckle draggers, but King Plumbing seemed like a professional, sophisticated organization.

"You can complete this and bring it by at your convenience. Just don't wait too long, because June will be here before you know it and we generally fill all of our academy slots," said Stephanie with a smile. "Now, let's go meet Mr. King."

Stephanie led Jim to a large, glassed-in office. He recognized John King from the ads. The man was large and somewhat heavyset, with a jovial expression. He paced energetically while talking on the phone. He waved them into the office and, as he finished his call, he walked over to Jim, thrust out his right hand, and grabbed Jim's forearm with his left for a two-handed shake. "You must be Jim. Come on in and take a seat. I've got it from here, Steph," he said.

"Uh, yes sir," said Jim. He found it impossible not to like the man instantly.

King smiled broadly and dove right in. "Do you know why you want to be a plumber?"

"Uh, no sir. Why?"

"Because every mother wants her daughter to marry a doctor or a plumber."

"What?"

"Think about it. Mothers want the best for their daughters. Both doctors and plumbers are useful. And both make good money. Well, both *can* make good money. A lot of plumbers don't realize how important they are to the world, but I do. And all of the plumbers at King Plumbing do."

"What's good money?"

"I'm glad you asked." King nodded at the big window fronting his office. One of his plumbers, wearing khakis and a King Plumbing polo walked by. "Take Jerod there. He's 25 years old and he's on track to easily break a hundred thousand this year."

Jim's jaw nearly hit the floor. Was it really true? He had no idea that plumbing could be so lucrative.

Contractor Stories

King launched into the importance of plumbing to society and how there would always be a need for plumbers. He talked about the freedom and independence that comes from operating a service truck. He talked about career opportunities. Then he talked about the academy and everything Jim would learn.

"There's only one catch," said King. "If we take you through the King Plumbing Academy you agree to work for us for two years. We're going to invest quite a bit of money in teaching you the plumbing profession. If you quit before the two years are up, you'll owe us for a portion of the training. If we decide you won't cut it, no harm and no foul. You keep what you learned and won't owe us a thing."

"How many people wash out?" asked Jim.

"Oh, probably 30% of the class won't make it to the end. And that's okay. It just means this wasn't the right profession for them. It's better to end the relationship sooner than later. So, what do you think?"

"I think I've got a lot to think about."

"Well, let me give you something else to think about. Once you learn a trade, you can always fall back on the trade. You might decide you want to go to college down the road. Plumbing can help you pay for it. It's how I paid for school. The old man wasn't going to help."

"You went to college?"

"Yes. I have a degree in finance. You see, I didn't start King Plumbing. Dad did. I thought I wanted to get as far away from the trade as possible. I thought a finance degree was the ticket to a nice desk job in an air-conditioned office."

"And?" asked Jim, fascinated with this turn in the conversation.

"And I made more money working for Dad as a plumber," laughed King. "I didn't like being broke, so I picked up my tools and asked Dad for a job. Over time, I bought the company from him and slowly began applying what I learned in school and what

I learned from attending conferences and from an alliance of plumbing contractors. King Plumbing took off. Now my biggest challenge is growing my team, which is why I'm talking with you."

***

Jim went home and reviewed all of the material Stephanie had given him. King Plumbing Academy sounded like an interesting opportunity. They would teach him how to troubleshoot and repair plumbing problems, how to interact with customers, and even how to manage his personal finances. It seemed to Jim that he would get more practical knowledge from KPA than from college. Plus, he wouldn't have to deal with politics. He took the tests and filled out the applications.

***

Two years later, his buddy Dale was home for Christmas. "Duuude," said Dale when Jim pulled up in front of his parents' house. "Nice ride."

Jim looked at his new F-150 Raptor, smiled, and shrugged. "I like it."

"So what's it like," asked Dale, "plunging people's toilets?"

"It's not what you think. What I do is really important. Today, for example, I went to look at a water heater that kept turning off. It turned out some idiot had blocked the vent. I'm pretty sure I saved a life or two today."

"What? How?"

"Well, the vent is supposed to remove carbon monoxide," answered Jim. When he could see Dale still wasn't getting it, he added, "You know, the clear, odorless gas that's a byproduct of gas combustion and can kill you quickly?"

"I guess."

"So what are *you* up to?"

"I just finished my finals, staying up all night studying stuff I'll never use. I have to take calculus next semester," Dale said as he rolled his eyes. "Can't wait."

"We have to use a fair amount of math in plumbing, though a lot of guys just use rules of thumb. Everything we use is practical. Since I'm mostly in service, I don't do as much as the new construction plumbers and the commercial guys."

Dale looked at him like he was an alien. "Hey, let's go grab some beer. Tech is playing in a bowl game. Let's kick back at the parental units' place with a couple of brewskis and watch it."

"Why don't we go to my place," asked Jim. "Your parents' TV is kind of small. I've got a 72-inch with surround sound."

Dale just stared. "What?" asked Jim. "I make pretty good money."

Over Dale's Christmas break, Jim spent less and less time with Dale. They lived in different worlds. It seemed to Jim that college was like a halfway house towards adulthood and Dale wasn't growing up. Meanwhile, Jim had become a much more serious person.

As he thought about it, Jim realized he had shouldered a lot of responsibility. He drove a company truck worth tens of thousands of dollars filled with nearly ten thousand dollars of inventory. While he reported in after every call, he was largely working on his own unless he ran into something he needed help with.

After graduating from King Plumbing Academy, Jim moved out of his parents' house and was on his own. While he was spending money, he was also saving it. Yes, he was given a lot of responsibility, but he was also independent and enjoyed a sense of freedom his friend Dale couldn't comprehend.

Jim thought about the decision he had made. His friend was in college, amassing a pile of debt and, it seemed, learning little practical knowledge. Jim had started a career, one that he really enjoyed, and was learning a lot about his trade and life. Not only was he largely debt-free, but he also had money in the bank. If he wanted, he could always go to college down the road. For now, the decision to join the plumbing profession seemed like the right one to Jim.

Why Start in the Trades?

- Learn a trade you can fall back upon.

- No college loan debt.

- Learn practical knowledge.

- Start making money sooner.

- Keep college as an option.

4

Why

Willie McGarn looked forward to the monthly local association meeting of his fellow contractors. He thought the programs could use a little spicing up, but they were just icing on the cake for him. This was a chance to discern how other contractors in the area were doing. For himself, Willie wasn't doing well. He was close to hanging it up and shutting the doors.

When he arrived at the hotel where the meeting was held, he headed to the bar. Sure enough, other contractors had already arrived. As he approached he heard the unmistakable drawl of big Sam Henderson. "Well if it ain't Willie McGarn! How you doing, Willie?"

"Hi, Sam," said Willie, dodging Sam's question. "How are you?"

"Why if I was doing any better it would be illegal."

"I certainly see enough of your trucks around town. If you don't mind my asking, how do you do it? No matter what the weather or economy, you seem to truck along."

"Well," said Sam, "Why don't you drop by one day and I'll show you my operation."

Willie couldn't believe what he was hearing. Sam Henderson was one of the most successful contractors in the area; heck, in the state! And he was willing to let one of his competitors see his operation from the inside? No way. Willie decided to call his bluff. "I'd love to see your shop."

Sam pulled out his phone and began scrolling. "How about Friday morning? I usually head out to the deer lease on Thursday, but Wilma's got me going to some performing arts thing Friday night and threatened me good if I tried to skip out."

"Uh, sure," gasped Willie. "How about nine a.m.?"

"See you then, brother. Now, what kind of program are they having tonight? I hope it's something more interesting than that guy from the city permitting office we had last month."

***

Sam pulled into the Comfort Commander lot and parked in one of the spaces marked for visitors. He wondered what people would think seeing his gleaming white McGarn Air truck in front of half a dozen of Sam's green-and-black Comfort Commander trucks. *Probably think I'm getting purchased,* he thought.

He entered a small foyer and pressed a button next to an intercom. "I'm here for an appointment with Sam Henderson," he said to no one he could see.

"Well come on in," a woman's voice answered and the door buzzed.

Willie pulled it open and walked through. What he saw was amazing. The large, open office was buzzing with activity. Lots of people with headsets faced large computer screens, talking with customers. The screens danced with schedules and time blocks. Others looked at different data entry or accounting screens, Willie wasn't sure which. Large LCD screens on the walls displayed company key performance indicators, salesperson rankings, technician rankings, and so on. One screen cycled through customer reviews.

A woman rose from one of the desks to greet him. "Hi. You must be Willie McGarn. I'm Patty, the office manager. I was told to expect you."

"I am," said Willie. "Thanks."

"Follow me and I'll take you to Sam."

Sam was seated in a glassed-in office at the very end of the hall. The room was paneled in oak, boasting a well-appointed bar, conference table, and battleship desk where Sam sat. Several hunting and fishing trophies were mounted on the walls.

"Hello, Willie," said Sam, coming around his desk and motioning to the conference table. "Have a seat. Want coffee?"

"No thank you. I'm fine."

"Let's chat for a few minutes, then I'll take you on a tour."

"Sounds good to me," said Willie.

While they talked, Sam essentially told Willie everything about his company. He shared his sales, margins, profitability, average service ticket, average installation, and on and on. Sam couldn't believe he was being so open. On the tour, he showed Willie his training room, technician lounge, meeting rooms, warehouse, including his stocking system, and let him listen to a call between one of his service managers and a technician who was on the job. Willie was fascinated with all of it.

As they headed back to the office, Sam stopped at a large printer and said, "Hey, look at this. This is my new toy. It prints vehicle wraps."

"You mean, you print your own wraps?" asked Willie, in awe.

"Yeah, why not? Buying the printer is easy to cost-justify and we've got enough trucks. I switched to our wrap design a few years ago. It was hard to swallow the cost at the time. I realize now it wasn't a cost at all, but one of the best investments I've made. Comfort Commander trucks pop. They are distinctive. Because of our trucks, we've got the best brand awareness of any HVAC company in the area. You should wrap your trucks. No offense, but one white truck pretty much looks like another white truck. It'll make a big difference in your business, I promise."

"I'll think about it," remarked Willie, who hadn't really thought about it before.

"Heck," said Sam. "With this thing, I'm thinking about wrapping furnaces and maybe even condensing unit caps. I can make mine look different and maybe even charge more. If I ever get into plumbing, I'm sure as heck going to wrap water heaters and disposers."

***

"So what do you think?" asked Sam when they returned to his office. "What are your questions?"

"Wow, I'm a little overwhelmed. I mean, you've opened up some possibilities I never considered. You know they don't teach this at the trade school."

"Don't I know it. Too many guys in the trade know more about turning a wrench than turning a profit. It's why they price so stinking low. And 'cause they price so stinking low, they can only afford to provide a stinking level of service."

"I might be one of those stinking guys."

"Well heck, son. Change. It ain't hard. What are you charging? Wait, no, don't tell me. For some reason, it's illegal for us to compare prices. But we can talk in generalities. I can give you my pricing calculator. Punch in your numbers and it'll tell you what you should charge. Low pricing is the single most common problem in the trade. It's also the easiest to fix."

"I don't get it," blurted Willie. "Why are you sharing all of this with me?"

"What do you mean?"

"Well, I'm your competitor," said Willie, before stopping at the blank look on Sam's face.

Sam stared at Willie for a second, then burst into laughter. "Son, you're not my competition."

"I'm not?"

"For starters, which one of my satisfied customers are you going to take from me? None of them. The only way one of my customers would ever consider your company was if I screwed up. If I did a crappy job and then blew the service recovery, I might piss 'em off so bad that they would look for someone else, at which point they would no longer be my customer."

"I guess that makes sense."

"And take someone who's a prospect-at-large. Do you know who my competition is for that guy?"

"Other air conditioning contractors."

"Nope. Given the price of a new system these days, my competition is anyone who offers something more compelling in the same general price range. My customer is the spa guy or the four-wheeler guy, or the river-cruise vacation guy. They all want the same 15 to 25 thousand I want and their offering is a heckuva lot sexier than mine."

Willie had never thought of it that way, but he could see Sam was right. "But," he interjected, "no one can live without air conditioning, right?"

Sam grinned. "Right. So while my competition might win this year or the next, there's a finite limit to how long we can keep an old system working. Sooner or later the customer will be mine and I'll make his life better, not for a few months a year, or for a week, but for years and years."

"Makes sense."

"But let's get back to you. How are you doing?"

"Not well," Willie confessed. "Maybe it's me. It just all seems so hard."

"Then do something else."

"What?" asked Willie. Of all of the things Sam could say, this was the last thing he expected.

"You spend most of your waking hours at work. Life's too short to spend most of the time doing something you hate. Do something else."

"I don't know anything else."

"Why did you get into air conditioning?"

"Dad was a refrigeration mechanic. He told me air conditioning was where it's at and I should go to trade school, so I did."

"That's why you started. Why are you still in it?"

"Like I said, I don't know anything else," said Willie. He felt a little defensive. Was this why Sam asked him here, so he could talk him out of the business and reduce the number of contractors?

"Let me tell you why I'm in it," said Sam. "I'm older than you are. I grew up in the South in a big old, historic house that was constructed in the twenties. It didn't have air conditioning. My parents were proud of the house, but either didn't have the money to retrofit it or weren't willing to spend it. Three rooms had window units. One was my parents' room. I shared a room with my brother. When he got asthma, we got a window unit for our room but were only allowed to use it at night. The third was in our TV room. Guess where we spent all of the time?"

"The TV room," Willie answered.

"Right. The TV room. In this big old house, we spent all of our time crammed into one of the smallest rooms because it was cool.

The rest of the house was hot and muggy most of the year. The smell of mildew was everywhere."

Sam continued, "You see, for me, this business is more than a way to make money, though I do that. It's like a calling. People are miserable when a Comfort Commander truck shows up at their house and comfortable when we leave. We keep people cool in the summer and warm in the winter. We represent a good night's sleep. We contribute to home safety because air conditioning makes it possible for people to close their windows and lock their doors. Most people literally could not live in this town without air conditioning. What we do is important and we're darn good at it."

Hearing Sam describe the industry, Willie felt better about himself and what he did. He could hear the passion in Sam's voice and see it in his eyes.

Sam paused, then said, "Sorry, I get a little carried away. But that's only part of it for me. I'm also here because of my team. I love to see people develop and grow. Now, how about you?"

"I... I don't know."

"Son, that's your problem. It's your biggest problem. Figure out why you're in business and other things will start to fall into place."

Willie thanked Sam and left. He had a lot to think about.

***

Willie asked himself, why was he in business? And why HVAC? The easy answer was to make money, but that seemed insufficient. He could make money in lots of ways besides HVAC. Given his total take-home, he could probably make the same or more working for someone else. Plus, he wouldn't have the hassles of all of the government paperwork. So why was he doing what he was doing?

His train of thought was interrupted by the phone. "McGarn Air, Willie here."

It was Sheila, his wife, dispatcher, and CSR. "Willie, we've got a no cool and Jim and Dave are both tied up. The customer sounds like she's up there in years. Can you take it?"

"Sure," said Willie. "Text me the address."

***

Willie rang the doorbell, stepped back, and put on his game-face smile. A short woman, her gray hair pulled back into a tight bun, answered the door. Perspiration dripped off her face as she fanned herself with a hand fan. "Oh, thank the Lord you're here. I think I'm going to die of a heat stroke. Come on in. Come in."

"Yes, ma'am. Can you tell me what the problem is?"

"Lord, I don't know. It just won't get cool. I think I'm going to die of heat stroke," the woman repeated.

"Okay, let me take a look. Don't worry," reassured Willie. "One way or the other, I'll get you cool today."

Willie started his diagnostic process. It didn't take him long to zero in on the problem: ants in the contactor. He told the old woman what the problem was and recommended replacing the contactor.

"Do whatever you have to do," she said. "My son and grandson will be here for a visit this afternoon. I don't know what I would have done if I couldn't get the house cool. Thank you so much."

When Willie gave the woman the invoice after he finished, she looked sort of startled. "Is something wrong?" he asked, certain she was going to complain about the price. They *all* complained about the price.

"No, there's nothing wrong," she said, handing him a credit card. "Why don't you add 20 dollars to the bill as a tip."

"You don't have to do that, ma'am."

"No, I want to. You've saved my family's visit and made such a difference."

***

At dinner that night, Willie said to Sheila, "You know, I went by Comfort Commander today."

"So you told me."

"Well, I've been thinking."

"Uh-huh," said his wife, eyeing him skeptically.

"Yeah, I know. It's dangerous for me to think too much. But I've been thinking that maybe we need a price increase."

"We've raised prices every time the manufacturers jacked up equipment pricing."

"I'm not talking about that. Well, maybe I am. But I was really thinking about raising the labor component of our service pricing. I guess I'd do the same for replacement prices."

"How much are we talking about?" asked Sheila.

Willie told her and watched while she made mental calculations. "Do you really think we could get that?"

"Yeah, I think we're probably underpriced. I mean, what we do is important. We make people's homes cool in the summer. We ought to get rewarded for it."

Sheila smiled. "Do you know what a difference this could make?" She opened the calculator app on her phone and punched in a few numbers. "My gosh, Willie, we could pay down our credit cards. By the end of the summer we might even have enough to take a real vacation. It would be a short one, but it would be a start."

***

The rest of the week was busy. Between running service calls and babysitting his techs, Willie didn't have time to think about

Contractor Stories

Sam Henderson's challenge to him. Saturday morning, Willie woke around 4:00 a.m. with a start. He sat straight up in bed. That was it. The old woman said it. His wife said it.

He got out of bed, grabbed a notebook, and started writing. When he finished, he leaned back, read what he wrote as a stream of consciousness, and smiled.

Yes, he thought. *This is why I do what I do. I can make a difference. I have a purpose beyond simply running service calls and selling replacements for old equipment.*

He marveled how uplifting this one revelation was to him. He couldn't wait to get to the shop and start working on ways to make a bigger difference.

Why I Do It

The reason why I'm in business is to make a positive difference in people's lives. I will make a positive difference in my customers' lives through the work the company performs by improving the comfort and air quality of the buildings where people work and live. I will make a positive difference in my employees' lives by giving them meaningful work, fair pay, and opportunities to grow and advance according to their desires. I will make a positive difference in my family's lives through the profit the business generates so they can enjoy an elevated lifestyle with tangible rewards and rich, intangible experiences that help us enjoy fulfilling lives. I will make a positive difference to the best of my ability.

5

The Start of Plumbing Season

The plumbers of Lombardi Plumbing crowded into the training room. It was early. Most of the public was still asleep or just starting to rise for the day. This was life for the plumbers. They were at the shop by 7:00 a.m. to attend a service meeting and get their trucks restocked.

Danny Jameson sat next to Buddy Baker. Buddy was one of the old hands and Danny was one of the newbies, assigned to work with Buddy.

Vinnie Lombardi walked in holding a pipe wrench which he set on a table. Buddy groaned a little. "Here we go again."

"What?" asked Danny.

"He does the same thing every year," said Buddy.

Vinnie interrupted, saying, "Buddy, why don't you get us started?"

"Yes, sir," said Buddy. "Everyone, let's face the flag. Join me in the Pledge of Allegiance."

The room rose to their feet in unison. Everyone put their right hand over their heart and joined Buddy. "I pledge allegiance to the Flag of the United States of America, and to the Republic for which it stands, one Nation under God, indivisible, with liberty and justice for all."

"Thank you, Buddy," said Vinnie. He liked to start every service meeting with the Pledge. Vinnie was patriotic and, like many in the service trades, a military veteran. He liked to remind his team that they were fortunate to live in the United States.

Following the Pledge of Allegiance, Vinnie had everyone recite the company's mission statement in unison: "At Lombardi Plumbing, we put our team first so they can put the customers first and protect the health and sanitation of our community."

After they finished, Vinnie held up the pipe wrench. "Gentlemen, and Lady," he said, with a nod to Jen Franks, the company's female plumber, "this is a pipe wrench." Most of the plumbers in the room joined in, finishing the sentence.

"All right," laughed Vinnie, "you've heard it before. Well, you're going to hear it again because our business is built on good fundamentals."

"So, is this a technical class?" whispered Danny to Buddy.

"Nah, just wait."

"All of you are good mechanics, even though experience levels differ. If you weren't you wouldn't be here. The problem is every service call involves broken plumbing and a broken customer. If you don't take care of the customer, you've only made half a repair."

Vinnie continued. "What this means is we need to make the people feel comfortable when we arrive, assured they called the right plumber, and delighted when we depart. This starts with our appearance. You guys know we belong to a business alliance. Every other year, they survey the customers of their members, including ours. That's a lot of customers. Anyone guess what the most frequently mentioned concern about plumbers for our customers and the country as a whole is?"

"Showing up late," shouted Danny.

"That's a good one and it sure is important, but it's not the most frequently mentioned, especially by our customers. Does anyone know why showing up late is less of an issue for us than the country as a whole?"

"We're fast drivers," said one of the plumbers.

"Better not be," cautioned Vinnie. "Remember, if you speed I get an alert from GPS. The reason we show up on time isn't due to your efforts. It's due to our dispatchers. Be sure to thank them from time to time because, without their skill, you would show up late more often. And what's it like when you show up late?"

Buddy jumped in. "The customer is irritated and cranky."

"And we all know how much Buddy likes cranky customers," said Vinnie, eliciting laughter all around. "But back to the most frequent concern. Any ideas?"

Vinnie looked around the room. "It's poor grooming."

"Grooming?" asked one of the plumbers.

"Grooming. Tell me, what's the stereotype for a plumber?"

"Three hundred pounds, shirt untucked, greasy hair under a dirty cap, and a butt crack," offered Jen.

"Exactly. Customers are letting you into their homes. Their homes! When you show up neat, clean, and professional, you are showing the customer a sign of respect. It's respect for the customer and it's respect for yourself."

"Some of our customers need a little self-respect," said one of the plumbers.

"Remember the lady who wouldn't throw anything away?" asked another with a shudder.

Vinnie regained control of the conversation. "That's true, but even a customer who lacks self-respect deserves *our* respect. These are the people who keep the lights on here and who allow us to

Contractor Stories

feed our families. So, every morning, I want you to shower, shave, except for you Jen, tuck in your shirts, and show pride in your appearance. Every person here represents the entire company when you're out *there*."

"When you show up looking sharp, the stereotype goes out the window and the customer says to herself, 'Wow, these Lombardi guys are different.' So, what else matters?"

"Parking," said Buddy. "Park at the end of the drive so the truck doesn't obstruct traffic, but get permission from the customer to leave the truck there and move if asked."

"Yes, sir," said Vinnie. "And when you park at the end of the drive, perpendicular to traffic, you maximize the exposure of our beautiful vehicle wraps to more people."

Vinnie looked at Danny. "What do we do next?"

"Um," said Danny, shifting in his chair. "Uh, breath spray?"

"Nailed it," said Vinnie to a beaming Danny. "We want to look sharp and we want to emit no odors whatsoever."

"Aw, come on," said Jen when the plumber next to her loudly passed gas, causing everybody else to crack up. "Don't tell me you've been saving that up."

"Who? Me?" the guilty party replied innocently.

"Okay, smart guy," said Vinnie. "Or should I say *fart* guy? What's important in how we interact with the customer?"

The plumber rolled his eyes but knew the company processes cold. He said, "We want to respect anyone with a concern about the virus by keeping our distance and asking if the customers want us to mask up, even though dispatch had already told us, and only very weird, very paranoid people want to wear masks these days..."

"They are still customers," cautioned Vinnie. "Continue."

"We want to make eye contact, smile, and nod to acknowledge the things the customer tells us and repeat them back to make sure we got it right."

"And," added Vinnie, "we always want to thank the customer for the opportunity to be of service. Remember, the customer pays for everything around here. The customer pays your paycheck and mine. She pays for your trucks, tools, insurance, and training. The more ways we can serve the customer, the more the customer pays us. How can we do that?"

Danny's arm shot up. He said, "We ask questions and present options. We never decide for a customer. We let customers choose to repair a problem, replace a product, or upgrade."

Vinnie smiled and nodded in acknowledgment. Then he held up an invoice. "What do we call this?"

"Paperwork," was the shouted answer.

"Do we ask the customer to sign the paperwork?"

"No," said one of the plumbers. "We ask them for their approval or authorization."

"Excellent," said Vinnie. "We want to use soft language and avoid terms like paperwork, signatures, and signing. And we want to conclude every call by asking if there is any other way we can be of service, thanking them for their business, reminding them of the importance of referrals, and finally, as a personal favor, because your boss measures you on this, ask them to scan the QR code to provide a review."

Vinnie wrote his list of fundamentals on the board. "Now," he said, "let's get outta here and go serve some customers!"

Soft Skill Fundamentals

1. Neat and clean.

2. Odor-free.

3. Park at the end of the driveway with permission.

4. Respect customer health concerns.

5. Make eye contact.

6. Smile.

7. Actively listen.

8. Confirm understanding.

9. Ask questions.

10. Present options.

11. Never decide for the customer.

12. Use soft language.

13. Thank the customer.

14. Ask for a review.

6

Everybody Sells

Ben adjourned the weekly service meeting and watched his technicians gather in the parking lot for the *unofficial* service meeting. This is where the grumblers grumbled, the gripers griped, the gossipers gossiped, and the no-drama guys pushed through to focus on getting their jobs done.

Mountain Air, Ben's company, had recently embraced a "connected home" strategy that allowed customers to buy thermostats, water alarms, water shut-off valves, cameras, light switches, door and window sensors, door locks, and garage door openers that were all linked through an app the company had white labeled. By integrating connected home monitoring with the company's standard air-conditioning service agreement, Mountain Air could offer total service to its customers that prevented breakdowns, stopped some home disasters, and increased peace of mind. For Mountain Air, it securely tied customers to the company, added to the product offerings, differentiated the company from competitors, and created a recurring revenue stream that would give the company a secure future against the private-equity-owned contractors. The only problem? Ben's techs were simply not offering it.

All he wanted was for the guys to hand the homeowner some literature and answer questions, but he wasn't getting any traction. Was it a problem of understanding the products and the consumer benefits? He didn't think so.

Bennie, the service manager, walked into Ben's office. Ben looked at him. "Any idea what the buzz is?"

"I think it's a couple of things," said Bennie.

"Like what?"

"First, they just aren't comfortable talking about it, so they don't. If one of them took the lead, the others might follow."

"And?"

"And you're asking them to sell. That's a four-letter word for technicians."

"Damn it," said Ben. "I'm not asking them to sell. I'm just asking them to talk about it."

"They see it as selling. They like the kits you gave them for their homes, but they're still reluctant to talk about it."

"Who do you think I've got the best chance of breaking through to?"

"Believe it or not, I think Tony's your best shot."

"Tony? He's the hardest case of all of them."

"And if we can get Tony to come around, the rest of them will too."

"All right. Tell him to come see me tomorrow morning."

***

Near the end of the day, after his last service call, Tony stuck his head in Ben's office. "You wanted to see me, Boss?" he asked.

Ben waved him in. Tony was a good-looking young man. He was clean-cut and presented himself well. He usually wore a smile and was the type of person other people warmed up to. Ben wished the rest of his techs looked as good as Tony did. He realized Bennie was right to pick Tony for multiple reasons. If Tony only tried halfway to talk about the connected home products, people would enroll in the program left and right.

"Have a seat, Tony."

"Did I do something wrong?"

"No, it's not that you've done anything wrong. It's what you *aren't* doing. Why don't you talk to customers about the connected home products?"

Tony shifted uncomfortably and broke eye contact. "Boss, I'm a technician. I don't sell stuff. It doesn't feel right."

"You never sell?"

"Never!"

Ben thought for a second. "Tony, you just got married a couple of years ago, right?"

"Yessir."

"And you've got a new baby?"

"Maddie's just turned six months," said Tony with pride.

"Your wife's Susan, right? How did you ever get her to go out on a date with you?"

Tony laughed. "Well, it wasn't easy. She's a manager at a convenience store. I started buying coffee there every morning. I had to persuade her to go to a Zac Brown concert with me."

"Persuade her?"

"She didn't want to go out with a customer. It wasn't easy. Zac Brown tickets helped."

"So you persuaded her, huh?"

"Yeah."

"You mean, you *sold* her on the benefits of a date with you. I thought you said you never sell."

"Aw Boss, that's not the same thing."

"It's not? Sounds like selling to me. Look, Tony, everyone sells. You just wait until your little girl grows up and y'all are at the store and she sees something she wants and tries to get you to buy it for her. I'll bet she'll be a really good salesperson."

"Probably," conceded Tony, thinking about how hard it would be for him to say no to his little girl.

"The problem, Tony, is you think sales is something you do *to* people. It's not. It's something you do *for* people. Did you know that Tom McCart, the first salesperson in our industry to sell a million dollars a year, way back in the 70s, had *Assistant Buyer* printed on his business cards? When someone asked him about it, he said his job was to help his customers buy the best comfort systems for their circumstances."

"Okay, but I'm not a salesperson. I don't want to be one. I'm a technician. If a system is really old and the repair is really expensive, I turn it over to Chuck or Todd, just like I'm supposed to."

"I know. And Chuck and Todd appreciate the leads. But that's beside the point. I want you to help people."

"I do help people," said Tony a little defensively. "I like helping people."

"I know you do. That's why I'd like you to let people know about our connected-home products. Heck, all you have to do is hand them the literature we give you and answer questions if they ask. You can even say, 'They make me give you this' when you hand it to them."

"It doesn't feel right. It's like we're trying to trick them or something."

Ben leaned back and thought for a second. He felt his phone buzz and touched a button on the side to silence it, then looked up at Tony. "Man, I love this phone. I remember when it was time to get a new one. I went online and read all these reviews on tech sites. I asked people about their phones. I knew that whatever I got, I would probably be stuck with it for a few years, and I didn't want to make a mistake."

"Yeah," said Tony. "I know what you mean. It gets really confusing."

"You know what I finally did?"

"Asked Barb?"

Ben laughed out loud. Barb was his wife and it was well known around the company that Ben pretty much did whatever she wanted. "I did actually. She wasn't any help. I ended up going to the phone store."

"Ugh."

"I walked in and asked for the guy who'd been there the longest. Turned out the 'guy' was a young woman named Jill. I asked her to explain the pros and cons of each phone. Do you know what she did?"

"No. What?"

"She started asking me questions."

"Like what?"

"She asked me what I did for a living. Then, she asked how I used my phone, where I used it, and how much I used it. She asked me what type of computer I used. She asked me what apps I used. She asked me about my budget. Only then did she start showing me the phones."

"She was selling you."

"Yes, in a way. I asked for the most experienced person because I wanted the person with the most knowledge. Jill knew her stuff. What she was really doing was helping me find the right phone for me, for my circumstances. I didn't really think of her selling me as much as helping me."

"Okay, but you walked into that. You were asking for it. Nobody is asking us about the connected-home crap."

Crap, thought Ben. *Man, this kid has an attitude.* He said, "You know why no one asks about it?"

Contractor Stories

"No."

"Because no one knows we offer it."

"Because we're a heating-and-air company, not a connected-home company."

"Actually, we're both. And who is better than us to talk with our customers about connected-home products? Do you think some kid with a few hours of training, cold calling door-to-door, knows anything about the comfort system? Thermostats are part of almost every connected home solution. How many times have you run into a screwed-up system because one of the connected home yahoos didn't understand HVAC controls?"

"A few," admitted Tony.

"That's one of the reasons we should be letting our customers know about what we can do."

"I'm just putting myself in the customer's shoes, Boss. I wouldn't want someone pushing these things on me, so I'm not pushing them on anyone else. You know, the Golden Rule: Do unto others and all that stuff."

"The Golden Rule works great until you run into a masochist," quipped Ben.

"A maso-what?"

"A masochist. Someone who seems to enjoy pain and suffering. You know, a Lions fan."

Tony chuckled, thinking about Bennie, the company service manager and a major Lions fan who went through agony every football season.

Ben said, "The Golden Rule is to treat people like you want to be treated. The problem is that everyone's not *you*."

"The world would be a better place if they were," answered Tony, deadpan.

Ben laughed. "Oh yeah. I can just imagine a world of Tonys."

Tony couldn't hold it and chuckled with Ben. "Okay, maybe the world's not ready for that much Tonyness."

"So instead of the Golden Rule, why not practice the Platinum Pule?" asked Ben.

"What's the Platinum Rule?"

"Treat people the way they *want* to be treated."

"How do I know how people want to be treated?"

"Ask them. Why do you think I ask everyone in the company to make a vision board?" asked Ben, referring to the individual vision boards along one hall of the company headquarters. Each vision board contained images of things or experiences the employee wanted.

Ben could see Tony was thinking. "The vision boards help me know how to help everyone achieve the things they want through the company."

Ben paused before continuing. "I want to add something else, but I don't think you're going to like it."

"What?" asked Tony a little defensively.

"Remember Francis, the tech I fired?"

"What about him?"

"What did he do?"

"He sold people stuff they didn't need, like when he talked that old woman into replacing a two-year-old heat pump. This is exactly what I'm talking about. This is why techs should never sell."

"Are you saying all techs are like Francis?"

"No. I'm not anything like that SOB."

"I agree. You aren't like him, which is why he's not here and you are. The old woman just wanted to be comfortable. The problem was inadequate return air. Francis knew that. I know he knew that, yet he never discussed it with her. The only choice he gave her was a new heat pump or nothing. What do you call that?"

"Dishonest. Unethical. Crooked," said Tony.

"How about arrogant?"

"Yeah, that too."

Ben looked away briefly and took a deep breath. "You know, you're just as arrogant."

"Me? What are you talking about?"

"Are you sure you can take it?"

"Yeah! I want to know how I'm arrogant," barked Tony.

"You're just as arrogant as Francis, but in a different way. You act like you know better than our customers do about what they want or don't want and what they need or don't need, so you never let them know what their options are, and what's available. That's making a decision for them. That's arrogance."

Ben watched Tony fume. This was touchy. If he handled this the wrong way, Tony would quit. That might not be a bad thing if Tony was influencing other techs the wrong way. Still, it was hard to find techs. Ben much preferred keeping Tony.

After letting him stew for a minute, Ben said, "I know you're mad. I just want you to think about it. And have I ever asked you to do something unethical?"

"No, Boss."

"So go home and think about what we talked about. Okay?"

"Okay, Boss."

***

Tony was mad. He wasn't quite *steaming* mad, but he was close. He thought about quitting. It would be easy to get a job with another company. But, he wondered, would it be any better?

Rudy left a year ago, telling everyone about all the money he was going to make. Reality differed. He didn't make much more than he did at Mountain Air. Plus, he worked his butt off. Rudy complained about the constant pressure to boost his average ticket. To a point, Tony understood the need. It cost a lot of money to position a fully stocked truck with a highly trained technician at a customer's house. Every extra dollar generated on a service call was important. But pressuring people wasn't something most techs wanted to do or were any good at.

When he got home, Tony greeted Susan, his wife, and went to check on his daughter, Maddie. She was in her playpen, batting at a mobile. Tony felt himself calm a little after watching his daughter. She was so cute!

Apparently, he wasn't calm enough for Susan. At dinner, she asked, "So what's up? Is something going on at work?"

Wives, he thought. It was like she could read his mind. "They're just pissing me off," he said.

"How?"

"Ben wants me to push the connected-home crap on customers."

"What do you mean, 'push?'"

Tony sighed. "They want us to hand out literature and talk to customers about it."

"Why not? It's awesome. At least, the stuff Ben installed here is. Whenever someone rings the doorbell and I'm at work, I can talk with the person through my phone. The thermostat automatically turns up when we both leave the geofence and turns down when one of us returns. That's saving us a lot of money on the power bill. Plus, I love the extra indoor camera because it helps me keep an eye on Maddie after I pick her up from daycare."

Tony just stared at his wife. When Ben unveiled the connected-home program, he had a manufacturer's rep work with every tech to install a basic package on another employee's home. The guys in apartments or rentals got a more limited package. Ben did the same thing with service agreements. Everyone in the company who owned a home had a service agreement, but techs weren't allowed to maintain their own systems because, as Ben says, they would never do it. Left to themselves, techs have the most poorly maintained comfort systems in town.

"Hello," said Susan, snapping Tony out of his thoughts. "Earth to Tony."

Contractor Stories

"We had setback thermostats before. I don't see how that saves us money."

"Pffft," said Susan. "We may have had them. We sure didn't use them. I don't think they were ever programmed."

Susan cocked her head at her husband. "Hey, wait a second. You haven't even opened the app, have you?"

"Sure I have."

"Hand me your phone."

"I'm not going to hand you my phone," said Tony, reaching for it.

Susan was too fast. She grabbed his phone, fiddled with it for a few minutes, and handed it back. "There, I've set it up so you get notifications on the app. You'll know when the doors open, when the doorbell rings, and when there's activity on the cameras."

***

The next day, while waiting at a stoplight, Tony heard a click on his phone. He glanced at the screen. The door to his garage had opened. Apparently, Susan was on the way to daycare with Maddie. About a half hour later he checked the app again and saw that, after Susan left the geofence, the setpoint changed to 82 degrees.

Throughout the day Tony watched the app. He saw a package delivered to his porch. When Susan returned home with Maddie, he was able to watch his daughter crawl around on the floor. He had to admit—grudgingly—that it was cool.

The next morning, Tony gathered his paperwork before approaching his first service call. He stopped for a second and, as an afterthought, grabbed the connected-home flyer, which he handed to the homeowner.

After the work was complete and Tony was collecting payment information, his customer, Mrs. Teal, asked him about the connected home. "Can you tell me about this?"

"It's some new stuff the company is offering. You know, cameras and sensors and switches and stuff. So, you can follow what's going on in your home."

"Does it work?"

"Yeah. I've got it at my home. Here, you can see where a guy dropped off a package yesterday," said Tony, showing Mrs. Teal the recorded video on his phone.

"What else can it do?"

"Well, we can put a sensor on your doors so you get a notification whenever they're opened."

"*Any* door?"

"Sure."

"My liquor cabinet door? I mean, I have a teenage son and believe in 'trust but verify' when it comes to teenagers."

Tony laughed, "Sure. We can do that."

***

Despite himself, three of Tony's customers bought connected home packages that week. Mrs. Teal was already a service-agreement customer so the service was added to her existing agreement. The other two bought the connected home/service agreement bundle.

When Ben saw Tony at the shop on Friday, he could hardly contain himself. "Tony!" he shouted. "My man. Getting some connected-home spiffs this week. Tell me what happened."

Tony knew this was coming. "Aw, Boss. It was like this: I hadn't really used the stuff, but Susan had and she loves it. She kinda sold me on using it and the product sort of sold itself after that. So, I admit, it's pretty cool and useful."

"Susan, huh?" said Ben. "Well, I guess it's true then. Everybody sells."

"Whatever you say, Boss."

***

Ben went back to his office. He tried to recall the conversation he had with Tony. The results were better than he expected. He grabbed his notebook and captured his thoughts.

Everybody Sells

- Selling isn't something you do to people. It's something you do for people.

- Everybody sells.

- Fundamentally, sales is helping people.

- The Platinum Rule is to treat people the way they want to be treated.

- Withholding information and options from customers is arrogant.

- Ultimately, sales is the transference of belief, and you must own a product to believe in it.

7

Fear

Jackson woke with a start. He looked around his bedroom, disoriented in the darkness, but gripped by irrational fear. He could see the soft glowing lights of his alarm clock. It was just after 2:00 a.m. His wife stirred as he quietly slipped out of bed. There was no sleeping now.

His sense of foreboding beat on him. He couldn't put a finger on the source. He went down a checklist in his mind. He made payroll Friday, though not by much. Still, it was progressing. He even paid himself.

The thought about payroll shifted immediately to his 941s, the IRS forms for payroll taxes. His heart skipped a beat, then started racing. He thought his bookkeeper paid them, but did she? He had heard from other electrical contractors that this was one of the places where embezzlement took place, and the IRS didn't care if you weren't the thief. You, as the company owner, were expected to personally make the government whole.

Crap. He couldn't remember signing the check.

He raced upstairs to his computer and checked QuickBooks. Whew, there was the entry. He leaned back, reassured, then sat bolt upright. *What if Sally forged the entry,* he thought with panic. *I need to check the bank account.*

Jackson tried to remember the password to his business account. The bank made him change it every three months and he couldn't remember what it was. *What if Sally changed it,* he thought? *What if she drained the account?*

After calming himself he remembered the password and checked the registry. There it was. *Thank goodness.* He felt better before feeling guilt and shame for his uncalled-for suspicions. Sally had never given him a reason to doubt her.

Crisis averted, Jackson still couldn't figure out why he was uneasy. He tried reading but found it hard to concentrate. It was now Sunday morning, so Jackson thought he should turn to the Bible. He thumbed it open at random to the 23rd Psalm, one of the most well-known in the Good Book. He didn't need to read it. He knew it by heart.

Yea, though I walk through the valley of the shadow of death, I will fear no evil: for thou art with me, he recalled from the King James Version. With a chuckle, he also recalled the version his unit used in the service before the possibility of engaging the enemy: *Yea, though I walk through the valley of the shadow of death, I will fear no evil, for I am the baddest mother fu…, uh, baddest mother in the valley.*

Why, he wondered, could he tamp down his fear when facing people who wanted to kill him, but not when facing the daily challenges of running a small business?

He opened his phone and read the latest news. Big mistake. There was bad news on every front. It seemed like the world was about to fall apart. The economy was teetering. Prices were up. Crime was out of control. The border was out of control. War was looming, including people openly talking about nuclear war. Seriously? The news just made him feel worse.

He finally gave up and tried to go back to sleep, but just stared at the ceiling until his wife's alarm went off. It was time to rouse the kids and get ready for church.

***

Jackson was distracted in his adult Sunday school class. He couldn't quite engage. David Solomon, another small business owner, picked up on Jackson's distraction. "Something the matter?" he asked simply.

Jackson shrugged. "I don't know. Maybe I'm not cut out for business."

"I thought things were improving?"

"Oh, they are. The problem is the more things improve, the more I worry. The more I'm afraid of blowing it. It's killing me. I guess I'm not like you. I don't know how you do it," said Jackson.

David looked at Jackson for a second. He turned to his wife. "Hey Barb, you mind if I pull Jackson from the service to help me with a prayer request?"

Barb nodded. "Of course." She looked halfway relieved that her husband was asked to get involved with a prayer request.

Then David turned to his wife and asked, "Okay with you, Hun?"

"Sure. And why don't we all go for lunch afterward?"

***

In a corner of the church coffee bar, Jackson asked David if he felt guilty lying about a prayer request.

"I didn't lie," David said. "I prayed that I'd be able to help you just before I said that. This is part of my prayer request. So tell me, what's up?"

Jackson sighed. "It seems like the more successful I become—and I'm not that successful, just keeping my head above water—the more I've got to lose. I mean, I could lose it all! I could lose everything I've worked on for years, everything I've sacrificed for."

David chuckled. "You don't think every small business owner's been where you are from time to time? Come on. You're not the first person to struggle under the burden of risk."

"Oh sure, like you've had problems."

"Brother, I've had more than my share of worries. For example, I had someone embezzle at least a hundred grand over a couple of years. This was someone I trusted. She created a false vendor account and paid her husband's fake business' fake invoices every month for two years."

"What? How did you catch her?"

"She got a bad case of the flu and I wouldn't let her snotty, infectious nose into the office. Made her go home. Otherwise, we might never have discovered her scheme. Stuff like this happens more than anyone wants to admit. We don't talk about it because we're all embarrassed to admit we've been such dupes."

"But you made up for it?"

"Not easily. We also discovered we were behind with a key supplier. In fact, they cut me off and I lost our main line of products. I had to switch brands. Man, I was terrified no one would buy what I considered a lesser brand of products from us."

"What happened?" asked Jackson.

"No one noticed. The only brand that mattered to our customers was *our* brand. I'd worked myself into a frenzy for nothing. Most of our worries as small business owners never come to fruition, unless we do something to help them along. Business ownership carries a burden and that burden never truly goes away no matter how successful you become."

"I don't know," blurted Jackson. "There's so much risk. So much responsibility. I mean, I've got eight families that depend on my company financially. That means they depend on *me*. I never asked for this."

"Yes you did," scolded David. "You asked for this the second you decided you weren't going to be a single truck operator, which was the right decision, by the way. If you were the company's sole employee, what would happen if you got in an accident and couldn't work?"

"I didn't think like that."

"Yeah, most small guys don't. What they don't consider is the risk to their family. One-truck contractors don't consider how selfish they are. That's part of the reason you build a company that can run without you. It can provide an income stream for your family if you can't work for months after having a quadruple bypass."

"Isn't that what happened to you?"

"Yes. And thank the Lord I put my company in a position to continue to operate while I was in a hospital bed."

"Okay," said Jackson. "How did you handle it when you were my size? How did you manage the pressure?"

"Now you're asking the right question. How do you think I handled it?"

"I don't know. Faith? Well, maybe my faith isn't as strong as yours. I read Job and the lesson I got is the guy had to go through a lot of pain."

"And yet, he kept his faith and emerged from the pain. Aren't you going through that now? A lot of pain?"

"Yeah," Jackson practically shouted. "I think of everything that can go wrong. Even when I can't pinpoint anything, I feel uneasy. It's killing me. I can't sleep. If one of my guys got in a wreck and killed someone the attorneys would take everything I own. I think of one of my guys touching the wrong wire at the wrong time and killing himself. I think about the work drying up."

Jackson continued, "I can't bear the thought of losing everything I've worked for. I can't bear the thought of letting my employees down, letting my family down. It's too much."

"No, Jackson. It's not. If you want to work for a paycheck, go ahead. Walk away. If you were a single-truck guy who didn't want to grow, I'd tell you to do exactly that, but you aren't. You're building a business that's more than a job. Give up at this point and you will always regret it. Yes, it's risky to own a business, but without the risk you wouldn't have the rewards. Most people choose safe paths. Less risk. Less reward. You wanted more. As a result, you risk more. It's something you have to accept and learn to live with."

"But the responsibility," complained Jackson.

"Yes, sir. You are responsible for the livelihood of other people. It's a burden that comes with the territory. Man up."

"What?"

David took a deep breath. "Do you read science fiction?"

"Are you kidding?"

"Okay, well there's a writer, Frank Herbert. He wrote the *Dune* books."

"Like the movie?"

"Yeah, like the movie."

"It's a crappy movie."

"Okay, but it's a good book. Anyway, Herbert used this line: 'Fear is the mind-killer.' What do you think he meant?"

Jackson thought for a second. "When you're afraid, you don't think. Your mind stops working."

"Exactly. Now, have you heard of Zig Ziglar?"

"The motivational guy. Sure."

"Ziglar said fear stands for *false expectations appearing real.* In other words, most of the things we worry about won't happen. There are all kinds of research studies supporting this."

"Okay, David. I might even be able to accept that. Waking up in the middle of the night with a panic attack doesn't do anything for me."

"So let's work it out. What's the worst thing that can happen to your business?"

"Easy. Bankruptcy."

"Then what?"

"What do you mean?"

"What would happen? What would your employees do?"

"They'd find new jobs, I guess."

"And how long would that take them in today's labor market?"

"I don't know. A nanosecond."

"Boom!" David practically shouted. "Everyone would get jobs. So they'd be okay. What about your family? What would you do?"

"I'd get a job somewhere or I'd start over."

"Let me ask you something. If you were approached by a licensed electrician who had run his own business and failed, would you hire him?"

"Absolutely!"

"Why?"

"Because he'd understand the economics of running a business better than most guys and know how hard it is, so he'd be less likely to leave... Okay, I see what you've done there."

David smiled. "Yeah, you would be a more attractive employee. You might be embarrassed about the business failure, but an employer would see your experience as an asset. The point is that the worst thing you can imagine would be survivable, right? *Right?*"

"I suppose."

"No, you don't suppose. You just said so. And if you can handle the worst case, you can handle anything else. It might not be fun, but you can handle it. So why worry?"

"Okay, I get that."

"There's a more important point. Have you heard of Earl Nightingale?"

"No."

"He was the first person to create a gold record based on the spoken word. It was called *The Strangest Secret,* and the strangest secret, the record's message, is this: *You become what you think about.* Denis Waitley is a psychologist who worked with Olympians and the space program. He said we all have a robot subconscious that we program and that it can't tell the difference between what we want and don't want. It just zeroes in on what we're focused on. If you focus on what you want, your subconscious mind goes to work to help you. If you focus on failure, it works the same way. Right now, my friend, you are focusing on failure. Stop it."

"Stop it?"

"Stop it. Change your focus. Focus on what you want, not what you don't want. Write down what you want. Visualize it. Focus on it."

"That easy, huh?"

"No, it's not easy. Listen, Jackson, I've been there. So have other people. They've been in worse places than you. Once, at an industry conference, I talked with a guy who took over his father's air-conditioning company. As he took the keys from his father, his dad said to put it in bankruptcy."

"That sucks."

"Not as bad as the crash Stan oversaw. He saw this company, this family legacy, go from operations in three cities and over a hundred trucks to two."

"Whoa. How did he manage that?"

"Perspective. His daughter had cancer as a child. For more than a decade he was in and out of hospitals with her. He told me that business wasn't hard. Watching his daughter go through cancer was hard. Watching a child die in the hospital elevator while he was on it was hard. He said I had no idea what was hard. He did and it wasn't business. A dead business can be rebuilt. A dead child is gone. Stan's message hit me hard. His message was to get some perspective. There were times when I needed it. You need it now."

Jackson felt small hearing about David's friend. He thought about his own daughter. Yeah, what he was worried about was nothing compared to what Stan had faced.

"There's another technique I use to deal with fear: Schedule time to worry."

"Huh?"

"Plan a couple of fifteen-minute segments where you'll worry yourself sick. Put them on your calendar. Don't let anyone interrupt you while you think about everything that can go wrong. Don't hold back. Worry, worry, worry. Then, when you start to worry or get afraid, tell yourself it's not time for that. You have to wait until the scheduled time."

"Fifteen minutes isn't enough."

"You think? I've found that I can't fill fifteen minutes without recycling the same worry. I can't do it. But if I don't guard myself, I can fill an entire day with the same five minutes of worry. Just try it."

"Okay. What else?"

"Release the sense that you're in control. Turn it over to God. You can only do what you can do. Quit trying to shoulder it all. Frankly, I'd tell you the same thing if you were a Buddhist or any other religion. Turn it over to a higher power. Stop trying to control everything yourself."

***

Jackson followed David Solomon's advice. It turned out Solomon was pretty wise. Go figure. As he focused on what he wanted in life and business, Jackson got control of his fear. Magically, it seemed to bring him success. It wasn't easy, but things were moving in the right direction. He started sleeping through the night. When he could recall the dreams he had during that brief period between sleep and wakefulness, they were no longer terror-ridden, but success-focused. The more he focused on success and the less he focused on fear, the more he received the former and the less he worried about the latter.

In his journal, the day after having coffee with David Solomon, Jackson wrote his recap about fear. He looked at it daily until he internalized the message.

Fear

1. I chose the risk and responsibility that accompanies business ownership.

2. Fear is the mind-killer.

3. Fear is *false expectations appearing real.* Most fears never materialize.

4. I can live with the worst case, so everything else is easier.

5. Focus on what I want. Think about what I want.

6. Keep perspective.

7. Turn it over to God.

8. Schedule time to worry.

8

Marketing

Gwen was having the worst day in the worst month of her life. Her marriage crashed before it really got off the ground. The divorce had just been finalized, but the breakup and stress had taken their toll. Her performance at work suffered and, today, she was let go. Freaking awesome. She stared at the kitchen counter in her tiny studio apartment and prayed for an answer. When her phone rang, Gwen nearly jumped out of her skin.

She looked at her phone and slid the answer icon. "Hi, Mom."

"I don't know why, but I just felt like reaching out and seeing how you're holding up."

"I've had better days. I got fired from the agency today. They said it was a layoff because of economic conditions, but that's not it. I haven't been carrying my weight."

"Oh dear. I'm so sorry."

"Well, I can't sit around and have a pity party. I need to find work. I can only make it about six weeks on savings."

"Dear, what about..."

"NO!" replied Gwen, more sternly than she intended. "I am not going to work for Dad. It'll never work and he won't listen to me."

"He's not doing too well either and I bet he could use your help."

"What do you mean?"

"He's stuck. The company isn't growing. He doesn't know what to do about it and he's too proud to admit it and ask for help."

"Okay. I'll talk with him, but no promises. I'm still getting my resume out there."

***

At dinner that night, Cheryl began working on her husband. "Mike," she said, "did you know Gwen was laid off?"

"What? No. I didn't know that. No one tells me anything."

"I'm telling you now."

"So what's she going to do?"

"I don't know. Look for a job somewhere."

"She's not going to move back in, is she?"

"Mike!" scolded Cheryl.

"I can love my kids without wanting them to live with us."

"I don't think she wants to move home. If she has a job, she won't have to."

"Surely someone will hire her."

"Hmm."

"Oh no," said Mike. "I know that 'hmm.'"

"Well, why not you?"

"Because one, we fight all of the time. And two, I can't afford her at the moment."

"How do you know you can't afford her?"

"Because she would be overhead, dead weight. I need more people in the field, not the office."

"I thought you needed more sales."

"I do, but if I get too much I'll need to add trucks. If I need more trucks, I'll need to pay for them. If I figure out how to pay for them, I'll need more guys in the trucks."

"What if Gwen can help figure all of that out?"

"Arggh," screamed Mike, throwing up his hands. "You aren't going to let this go, are you?"

"Just call her and talk with her. What can it hurt to talk?"

Mike sighed. He knew better than to keep fighting this battle. "Okay, I'll talk with her, but no promises."

Cheryl smiled, thinking father and daughter were so much alike and neither one knew it.

***

Gwen arrived at Ready Plumbing, Heating, & Air. After chatting briefly with Terry, the office manager, she headed back to Mike's office. She took a deep breath and walked in, closing the door behind her.

Mike came around his desk and gave his daughter a hug. "How're you doing, kid?"

Gwen shrugged. "There are good and bad days. I just seem to have misplaced the good days."

"Maybe that means you'll get them all at once. Have a seat," said Mike, sitting behind his desk.

"Hope so," said Gwen, dropping into the only chair that wasn't stacked with trade magazines.

"Your mother thinks I should give you a job."

"I don't want you to give me anything."

"Then why are you here?"

"Mom thinks I should help you hang up the phone on the eighties. Welcome to the 21st century."

"Well Cheryl can just…"

"Stop, Dad. We both know she means well and we both know she'll either get her way or drive us both crazy, so maybe we can work something out."

Mike leaned back. "So what do you propose?"

"I know marketing. I mean, I really know it. I know you're probably stretched pretty tight financially, so here's what I can do. Pay me minimum wage and a commission on the increased revenue from any changes you let me institute and any increased revenue I bring in."

"What changes?"

"I don't know yet, but I can't be battling you on everything. You've got to give me some rope."

"We don't have a lot of excess cash lying around to waste on marketing that doesn't make the phone ring."

Gwen reached over and picked up an oversized postcard from her father's desk. "And how much did you spend on this?"

"Too much for all of the good it did."

"You know why it didn't work?"

"Yeah, marketing sucks."

"No. It didn't work because a manufacturer designed it. It's all about equipment. Nobody cares about equipment. Well, I take that back. *You* care. Your territory manager cares. Your service techs care. None of your prospects care about equipment."

"What do they care about?"

"Cold air on a hot day. Warm air on a cold night. Hot baths and showers. Toilets that flush. Designer baths and kitchens. So, I give you that. They care about brass and porcelain, but they don't call it that. To your customer, it's décor."

"Who's my customer?"

"Who calls for service, the man of the house or the woman?"

"The woman."

"Who is there when your tech arrives, the man or the woman?"

"The woman."

"So there you have it. I'm your freaking customer or I will be in a few years. Yet you don't market to me, you market to yourself. Remember when you bought that radio package on the local sports-talk program a few years ago?"

"Yeah, everyone heard it, but it didn't make the phone ring."

"No, your friends heard it and they aren't your customers. You didn't care at the time because you got to meet Jose Whatever-His-Name-Is after a baseball game."

"That was pretty cool."

"Yeah, but you were advertising to yourself. Let's get back to this postcard. What did you spend on it?"

"Nothing. It was part of the program."

"You mean the one where you fork over five figures for the right to sell their product that none of your customers can tell apart from anyone else's product?"

"Well, uh..."

"Look, I can get some of the money I need right here with this," Gwen said, waving the postcard. "All this does is show me stuff and a sale sign. Every other dealer in the area probably used the same darn card."

"No, they were all customized."

"With what, your logo? And where is it?" Gwen studied the postcard. "Oh, here it is, right below the manufacturer's."

"That's brand association," protested Mike.

"That's bull," said Gwen. "You get co-op dollars from the guys, but the rules stink. Let me talk with them and I'll get them to free up your co-op to use for marketing that works."

Mike sighed again. Gwen was so headstrong. And so was Cheryl. He thought they were just alike, though neither one knew it. He decided discretion was the better part of valor. "Okay, you win. You need to find the money you want to spend, and run things by me before making changes. You run them by me in this office with the door closed. We agree or disagree, but when we walk out of here, we have to be on the same page as far as everyone else in the company is concerned."

"Really?"

"And I'll pay you better than minimum wage. You'll get 10% of the cash-on-hand increase each quarter."

"Cash? Not EBITDA?"

"Cash is easy to track. Cash is something I can use to pay bills. EBITDA involves accruals. I don't want accounts receivable. I want cash."

"Okay, Dad. We'll do it your way, but I want 30%. Wait. Stop. You don't have it now, so it's still a win."

"My own flesh and blood, robbing me blind," said Mike, shaking his head.

***

Gwen drove home and mentally kicked herself. Darn it! The last thing she needed was to be around her father. She loved the man, but he drove her insane.

Life already sucked. Now she was being drawn into the negative drama of the family enterprise, that is, if one used a loose definition of enterprise.

Deep down, she wondered if she was picking a safe option. No matter how much she battled her father, he wouldn't fire her. Gwen's mother would see to that.

And yet, she made the commitment. She couldn't back off now. Her pride—what was left of it—wouldn't allow her to. So if she was taking the safe option she might as well make the most of it. She could turn Ready into something worthwhile, something she could be proud of contributing to.

Mentally, she began outlining a very basic marketing plan. It consisted of two broad elements. Find money. Spend it cautiously, while growing more of it.

***

Three weeks later, Mike stared at the invoice. "What is this?"

"It's a business alliance with a buying group. Gwen enrolled us," replied Terry.

"Terry, will you step out for a minute and ask Gwen to come in?"

"Sure, boss."

When Gwen walked in, Mike said, "I thought you were going to run things by me?"

"This was a no-brainer."

"It's an expense."

"No, it's revenue, or will be next quarter. We'll earn rebates on purchases. It means we might have to change a couple of the products we buy and services we use, but it's like free money that I can use for marketing."

"How much money?"

"A lot. Plus, they'll give me help on my marketing and some other business forms. They'll help me with some of my social media posts."

"Social media?"

"Yeah. We have a social media presence now. It's building and you should like this: It's free until we start paying for ads, which I haven't yet. We're also pushing online reviews, which social media will help with. Besides, it's not like I've got a team of marketing people to help me."

Mike sighed. "Okay, we'll try it. For now."

"Oh, and I transferred your local chamber of commerce membership to me as the primary since you never attend the mixers. I also joined a service club and a leads club."

"Is that what these invoices are?" asked Mike, holding up another batch.

"Yes."

"So far, it's all been money out and no cash in."

"Not true. You know the system replacement Doug sold last night?"

"Yeah, the 15K one?"

"That was a direct lead from my service club. Doug also priced it for a 48% gross margin."

"What? How?"

"I raised his commission percentage based on the gross profit he brings in."

"I thought we were going to talk about stuff like this," said Mike.

"We would have, but you were fishing and you turn off your mobile when you fish. I do have something I need to run by you."

"Finally."

"Come on, Dad. It's not that bad."

"What do you want to do?"

"I want to raise service prices."

"How much?"

"Fifty percent."

"Are you crazy?"

"You're underpriced. It's one of the reasons you don't have any cash. Have you looked around? There's been a lot of inflation. You bumped equipment prices, but not service. You need to charge more and you need to pay more or you'll lose people."

***

A week later Mike pulled up to the shop, got out of his truck, and gaped. He stood open-mouthed, looking at one of his trucks. It was wrapped in purple with a cartoon sprinter at a starting line, holding a pipe wrench as a baton. The logo was huge. And tilted. Mike cocked his head slightly as he looked at it.

"Like it?" asked Gwen, walking out the front of the building.

"Office!" barked Mike.

Gwen trailed her father into the office. "Before you get all upset, I bartered with a sign company for this first one, so there was no cash outlay, though we did have a little labor and materials."

Mike gritted his teeth. "I... DO... NOT... LIKE... IT!"

"Really?" Gwen asked, genuinely surprised.

"REALLY!"

"Well, it's done now. Let's see what happens, then you can decide if you want to wrap more trucks. Come on, Dad. Just see what happens."

***

A week later Mike was enjoying a rare Sunday afternoon of golf with a couple of his buddies. At the 19th Hole bar, Stan declared, "I think Mike gets to buy. He's clearly doing well. I see those new purple trucks everywhere."

"Yeah, no kidding," added another buddy. "How many of those trucks do you have? It's gotta be five or ten."

Mike agreed to pick up the check, but kept quiet about the number of trucks. He had one purple truck. One. Yet everyone seemed to think he had five to ten times that number.

***

On Monday, Mike called to his daughter as he walked into the shop. Gwen rolled her eyes as she followed him to his office. "What did I do now?"

"How much does a truck wrap cost and how long does it take?"

"Come on, Dad. Give it some time. If we don't see results by the end of the year, we'll pull the wrap and put on some crappy decals."

"You don't understand. I want to wrap the whole fleet."

"Really? You like it?"

"I don't get it, but it gets noticed."

"It's not hard. Each truck draws 30 thousand or more impressions a day. That's 30 thousand. When all of your trucks are wrapped, the Ready brand will have greater brand awareness than any of the products you sell *just because of the trucks*. Plus, no one has the same color we're using, so we'll stand out and eventually own the color. Over time, the wraps will result in more phone calls and easier sales."

"I believe you. Now what else have you cooked up that you haven't told me about?"

"We just started radius marketing."

"What's that?"

"First, it's not like the manufacturer postcards. It's affordable, targeted, and effective. Plus, I'm using your manufacturer co-op funds to pay for it, so it is kind of free. We've designed a series of letters that get mailed to every hundred homes around every service call. We're also mailing out special offers to new homeowners."

"How are you getting the addresses?"

"We've hired a service to do it. They turnkey everything, so it doesn't take much time. Terry emails them the address of every service call at the end of each day and they do the rest for the radius marketing. They do the new homeowner marketing as they get the new homeowner lists."

"And what are the results?"

"To be honest, too early to tell, but I'm pretty sure this will be a home run. Every radius marketing letter has a good chance of hitting homeowners who share the same problem we just fixed for their neighbor, or they'll share it soon. The odds are good and it only takes one replacement out of a couple of thousand dropped to put us in the black. Plus, with so many marketers abandoning old-fashioned snail mail for digital, we'll have less competition in the mailbox."

"Okay, I'm sold."

"Good because I'm working on targeted cable-TV advertising next."

"TV?" asked an abashed Mike. He took a deep breath and added, "Given the leads we're getting from your personal community-networking activities, the complete lack of a pushback on the price increase, the apparent motivation from increasing incentives, the impact of the truck wrap, and the growing cash in the bank, I'm starting to think my daughter is a lot smarter than I am. Go for it."

"Thanks, Dad."

"There's only one problem."

Gwen sighed. "And what's that?"

"We're going to need more trucks and more people. We can afford the vehicles, but where are we going to get the people?"

"Recruiting is nothing more than a marketing problem. I'm already working on it."

***

Mike's CPA emailed him the year-end financials in January. It was the best year in his company's history. They grew by 20% and EBITDA was up by much more than that.

"Mike," said Cheryl. "We agreed, no phones at dinner."

"Sorry. I was just looking at the financials. I think it's time."

"Are you sure about this?"

"Yes. It's time."

***

When Mike got to the shop the next morning, he called out to his daughter. "Gwen, follow me if you will."

Once again, Gwen rolled her eyes while Terry suppressed a grin. When she got inside, she slumped down in the chair. "What now, Dad?"

"I don't think I want you to be our marketing director anymore. You'll need to get up. That's not your chair."

"What?" Gwen practically screamed. Things had been going so well. Things were working at the company. She was getting along with her father. She was getting by financially and had even had a few dates. In an instant, her crummy life before going to work in the family business, when she was newly unemployed, newly divorced, and felt like an all-around failure, came screaming back at her. How could her father do this to her? Her father! How?"

Mike watched the array of emotions flash across her face. "Your chair is on the other side of the desk. That's where the company president sits."

"You're firing me? I can't believe you're firing me. Wait. What?"

"I said the company president sits in this chair."

Gwen's eyes grew large as she realized what her father was saying. Mike laughed. "If you could've seen your face just now."

Gwen was half crying and smiling. "Dad, that wasn't funny. That wasn't funny at all."

Mike laughed so hard he had to sit down.

"Get out of my chair!" ordered Gwen.

Gwen's Marketing Plan

Find the Funds

- Raise prices.
- Use co-op her way.
- Use buying-group rebates.

Spend Carefully While Growing

- Network through community organizations and leads clubs.
- Execute social media and review sites.
- Incentivize higher-margin sales.
- Pick a unique color and professionally wrap trucks.
- Start targeted direct mail.
- Add targeted cable TV for top-of-mind.

9

Slump

The worst time in John's life was his senior year in high school. He got offers to play ball from D1 schools. The pros talked about drafting him. He led his American Legion league in batting average, hits, and RBIs. He was third in home runs. Then the slump started.

His coaches tried to help, but John was too proud. He felt he could beat it on his own. He couldn't. The slump continued... and continued... and continued. John went from lead-off to bottom of the lineup. Scholarship offers were quietly rescinded. The pros quit watching him. Eventually, he was benched. He got it. His starting spot was based on his bat, not his glove. When the season mercifully ended, so did his dreams of playing in college or the pros.

Now he faced another slump, a *sales* slump. This wasn't just a game, it was his living, his income. Comparisons between his sales career and his baseball career flooded his mind. Would his sales career end as unceremoniously as baseball had? It would if something didn't change.

It had been 14 days since John's last sale. That was two weeks without a close. It wasn't like he lacked opportunities. He had them. He just wasn't closing. As he sat across from Mr. and Mrs. Shipley, he felt another K, another strikeout, was coming. On a whim, he decided to offer the lowest price. *At least I won't be beat on price,* he thought.

As a comfort consultant, he had permission to drop his price, as long as he dropped his commission with it. He punched up a zero-commission sale, just to get himself on the board. "Mr. Shipley," he said, "I can offer you our budget system with no frills to save you the most money. You said saving money was important."

"How much does it cut our utilities?" asked Mrs. Shipley. "I don't want to pay any more money to the power company than absolutely necessary."

"It will save you quite a bit. And it won't cost a fortune," added John, noting that Mr. Shipley seemed to perk up at the thought of saving money. He slid the quote across the desk to Mr. Shipley.

As Mr. Shipley looked at it, Mrs. Shipley said, "Thank you. We'll get back to you after we've had time to talk about it."

Yup, thought John. Another K. And he swings and he misses. "Okay," he said, "Let me know. You've got my card."

***

John remembered how his baseball coaches tried to help, but he rejected them because he was too proud. Well, this was his income. He wasn't too proud now. If he didn't get help, he would be on unemployment. He asked himself who he could turn to. Bill Swenson came to mind.

Bill was an old-school territory manager, or TM, who called on John's company. He built a strong territory with a loyal dealer base.

At one point he jumped into the contracting game, then jumped out. Bill found it was much harder than he thought. His respect for the contractors grew accordingly. While he didn't excel as a contractor, he was very good at coaching the contractors he served. This included coaching the occasional struggling comfort consultant.

"I don't get it," John confided to Bill at a local coffee shop. "What's going wrong?"

Bill asked, "What do you *think* is wrong?"

"I don't know. It seems like people are scared about spending money. Plus, the equipment has gotten so darned expensive."

"Uh-huh. So how are the other guys doing?"

John sighed. "They're making sales."

"Same products, right?"

"Yeah."

"Same pricing, right?"

"Yeah."

"Same basic customers, right?"

"Okay, I get it."

"So what's the problem?"

"Me?"

"Well, son, I think that's the first step. Whose problem is this? And who is the only person who can fix it?"

"Me. I'm responsible."

"You're responsible. So, what can you do about it?"

"I don't know. That's the problem."

"Are you asking the perfect questions? Making the perfect presentation?"

"What?"

"Do you like golf?"

"Of course. What's that got to do with anything?"

"What does a professional golfer do when he starts hooking or slicing drives?"

"I don't know."

"He starts looking at his technique. What is he doing wrong? Baseball hitters do the same thing."

John stared. That's one of the things he didn't do in high school. He never studied his swing or his stance. How could he have been so stupid?

"Earth to John," said Bill.

"I need to record and review my presentation."

***

John videoed himself giving a presentation to no one in particular. It was bad. He had slipped into bad habits. He put his phone on record during a sales presentation and realized he was even worse under pressure. He was trying, but he lost two more sales. He realized he needed to watch someone doing it right. Bill couldn't help here. *Crap,* he thought. He needed Derek.

Derek was younger than John and newer on the job. But Derek was killing it, while John was not. It would kill him, but he knew he needed to ride along with Derek on a call and ask Derek to return the favor. *Crap, crap, crap!*

***

"Dude," said Derek, "I'll let you ride on a couple of my calls but you can't say a freaking thing. If you speak up and blow it..."

"I get it. I'm just there to observe. I'll owe you one," said John. It was hard for him to say. It was hard to show humility to a cocky freaking kid.

During the call, John was amazed by the confidence Derek showed about things he knew absolutely nothing about. Yet the customers seemed to feed off his brazenness. He never even asked for the order. He just started filling out the paperwork. The customer didn't stop him and he got the sale.

John asked Derek to ride along on one of *his* calls. Afterward, Derek told him, "Dude, you're acting scared. You're afraid of losing the sale instead of going for it. The customers feel your uncertainty and it's killing you."

The only thing harder than hearing the criticism from Derek was realizing he was right.

***

John was with Bill Swenson again in the coffee shop. "Okay," he said to Bill. "I've worked on my questions and worked on my presentation. I've recorded myself. I even rode along with Derek."

Bill spat out his coffee. "You rode with Derek?"

"He's been closing sales, so yeah. And he rode with me."

"And what did you learn?"

"That he doesn't ask for the order, he just writes it up."

"What do you mean?"

"We were right at the point where he was supposed to present options. He did. Then he said, 'I think this middle one is the best for you and your situation. It's so much per month using our main finance company. There won't be any approval problems will there? Great, let's get the paperwork filled out and I'll schedule the installation.'"

Bill leaned back. "Smart. Do you know the psychology he's using?"

"Not really."

"First, he's making an assumptive close. A lot of people feel overwhelmed today and actually *want* someone to tell them what to do. He does, but softly."

"Yeah, I guess I see that."

"Then," added Bill, "he does a sort of takeaway. It's like he challenges their creditworthiness, so they want to prove they

Contractor Stories

have good credit and proving it means applying for financing. As soon as they start filling out the information, he's closed the sale."

"Yeah, well, that style really isn't me."

"Then adjust it to something that *is* you. What else did you observe?"

"He does exactly the same thing on every call. He's almost robotic."

"You mean he's following a process."

"The same one I learned but got away from."

"You know what Nick Saban says about football?"

"Yeah, focus on the process and everything else takes care of itself. It's just... I've been in such a rut."

"So tell me, how did you go to work today?"

"Same way I always go."

"And what did you do for lunch?"

"Fast food."

"And yesterday?"

"Same."

"Do you see where I'm going?"

"Not at all," said John.

"You just said you're in a rut. A rut doesn't just affect one aspect of your life. It's everywhere. You drive the same way, eat the same stuff, watch the same TV shows, do the same thing on sales calls. You're in a life process that doesn't work. Change it. Change the route you drive. Change your lunch habits. Break out of the rut in one area and you'll break out in others. Try it."

John sighed, "Okay. Okay, I will."

"What did Derek say when he rode with you on a sales call?"

"He said I'm scared and the customers can sense it."

"Hmm," added Bill. "Okay, I want you to try a couple of other things. On your next sales presentation, don't worry about selling."

"What?"

"If you're going into this afraid, prospects will sense that and wonder what you have to fear. Now you and I both know it isn't the excellent products you're selling," said Bill, laughing.

John chuckled with him. "Yeah, can't be that. But the customer doesn't know that."

"Right."

"Next, skip the news. Avoid it like the plague. Economists have predicted ten of the last two recessions. Do not let the media make you pessimistic. Feed yourself positive material. Read Zig Ziglar or Jeffrey Gitomer or Simon Sinek. Take your pick."

"Okay. What next?"

"Call me after your next sale and I'll buy you dinner."

***

John changed his route home. Instead of take-out, he cooked his own dinner. Instead of watching the news, he picked up an old Denis Waitley book called *The Psychology of Winning*. Before he went to bed, he outlined every step in his sales process and visualized success.

The next morning, he was crushed to hear he wasn't getting any leads that day. "Leads go to the hot hand," his boss said. "Right now, that's Derek and James. We had two come in over the transom and they get them."

Instead of moaning about how terrible it was, John did what he could. He started calling every prospect he'd given a presentation to. If he didn't get something from them, he would go through old service invoices until he got a chance to get in front of a prospect.

John was surprised to learn that the Shipleys hadn't made a decision. "Why don't you come back over and let's talk," said Mrs. Shipley. "I want this darn thing replaced before it gets really hot and breaks again. But I don't want cheap. I want good. I don't want to deal with this again, ever."

John hustled over. He'd already lost this sale, so there was nothing more to lose. He might as well swing for the fences. *You can do this,* he told himself.

Mrs. Shipley greeted him at the door and led him back to the kitchen. Mr. Shipley was drinking a cup of coffee and offered one to John. John accepted, then surprised the couple with an apology. "Mr. and Mrs. Shipley, I want to apologize for my presentation the other day. I thought you might be interested in the cheapest option, but I don't think that's the best one for you. Let me show you what I recommend and go over the reasons why I think it's a great fit."

"Well, there's nothing wrong with a bargain," said Mr. Shipley.

"Hush," said Mrs. Shipley. "Let's see what he says."

***

Before John drove away he pulled out his mobile phone and dialed Bill Swenson. "Hey, Bill," he said. "I think I want a filet mignon tonight."

How John Broke His Slump

- He accepted responsibility.

- He identified and improved his poor technique.

- He rode along with a successful salesperson.

- He sought and received criticism for his sales approach.

- He focused on the process.

- He changed routines to break his rut.

- He eliminated fear from his mind.

- He avoided the news and read motivational books.

- He put in the work.

10

Family Business

Clay was finally getting over his anxiety about the acquisition of his employer, Komfort King. His boss and former company owner, Will Hayes, said everything would stay the same and, mostly, it had. There had even been improvements. The benefits were way better. The growing sense of comfort made it all the worse when the text message hit on Sunday night: "All Company Meeting @ 7:30 Mo. Attendance is Mandatory."

As soon as he saw it, Clay knew that, as a service manager, his own phone was about to light up. He texted Will to ask what was up. "No idea," came the reply. "Just got the same text u got."

Great. And right on schedule, his guys started asking what gives. He texted all of them. "Don't know what's up. Might not b bad. Might b good. Might b nothing." His gut told him it was something else, something bad.

***

Clay got to the shop at 6:30 a.m. as usual. He made coffee and started checking over the call board, even though it was no longer a "board" but part of their field-service software. He also jotted down notes for the service meeting, which he would start promptly at 7:00 a.m.

The techs were filing in, giving each other grief in the way they always did. Tony was showing everyone the picture of a buck he took Saturday morning, despite the fact he'd already texted it to everyone. Bill was taking it on the chin because the Lions lost on Sunday. He was good-natured about it. After all, the Lions almost always lost and Bill had learned to embrace the mediocrity.

Clay got everyone together and started going through his action items. He started with the supply-chain issues. He went over a callback, using it as a learning opportunity to review their diagnostic process. He had Tony talk about the features and benefits of a new UV light they were promoting as an add-on during cold-and-flu season. When Clay noticed the private-equity guys through the window of the training room door his stomach did a little dipsy-do.

The door opened and the two guys filed in, followed by Will. Clay interrupted Tony, who was doing a good job. "Guys," Clay said, "It's time for the meeting, the *other* meeting. Let's make some room."

The technicians scooted their chairs to the side. Some stood and offered their chairs to the CSRs and other office people who walked in a little bleary-eyed. Will walked to the front. "Everyone, this is Cooper Simmons and Smythe Lancaster from Riverrock, the company that bought us."

Clay noticed how everyone was shifting uncomfortably. Simmons and Lancaster didn't fit and it showed. They weren't the type of guys to hang out at the tavern after work to slug down a

Leinenkugel's over a game of pool or darts. They were the types who drank highly-rated wine that cost more per bottle than most of the techs earned in a day.

Simmons stepped up. "Good morning, everyone. First, let me express just how pleased and excited we are at Riverrock to have Komfort King as part of the family. It's a growing family and that means opportunities for everyone. This morning we will close on Comfort Commander. Smythe here will update us on how this will impact the Komfort King operation."

Lancaster took Simmons' place. Clay couldn't help but notice an innate smugness in his *Smytheness,* as he described Lancaster to himself.

Lancaster began. "First, in order to optimize our solution-execution structure within our business-line operations, we will consolidate our regional environmental solutions under the Comfort Commander established organization and utilizing their considerable brand equity. This is not only beneficial but necessary for advancing our actionable administrative framework, so that we drive further congruence in our executional structure, streamlining and gaining efficiency in marcom—that's marketing communications—and lending simplicity to our overall corporate and go-to-field operations."

Clay was struggling to understand what he was hearing and if he was hearing it correctly. Based on Will's stunned look, he was reading it right. The glazed-over looks of the rest of the team made it clear that no one had a clue what Lancaster just said.

Lancaster paused, smiled, and continued. "This action is critical to the establishment of a controlled operational approach, congruent with the need to align investment opportunities where robust executional outcomes are maximized to meet the EBITDA expectations we have set. Conversely, this necessitates the need for overhead and infrastructure optimizations to ensure we maximize the operational harvest in line with, if not in excess of, planned growth. Accordingly, the requirement for some to be transitioned out of the organization is necessitated and will be communicated later today."

Simmons stepped forward and nudged Lancaster's back. "Well, that's that. No one can lay out a complex institutional message quite as concisely as a Harvard MBA like Lancaster here. If there are no questions, we'll be off."

Bill raised his hand. "I've got a question. Just what the heck did he say?"

Everyone laughed. Simmons did as well, adding, "Good one, man. I can tell you are the wit of the operation."

Before anyone could say anything else, he turned and walked out of the training room and deposited himself in Will's office with Lancaster on his heels. Will mouthed to Clay, "Get them on the road."

Clay said, "Alright. Techs stay here for five. Everyone else get going." Amid the murmurs and grumbles, Clay announced, "Look, I don't speak Harvard any better than the rest of you. Let's just get to work and I'll get with Will. Now go!"

Clay watched the techs head out and reassemble in the parking lot. Meanwhile, he heard Will raising his voice in his office. He went to the warehouse and started taking inventory to keep his mind off of whatever the heck was happening.

***

An hour later, Will called Clay and Claudia, the office manager, into his office. He sighed. "You heard what the guys from Riverrock said."

"I heard," said Claudia. "I didn't understand."

"Well, here's the long and the short of it. We're going to be part of Comfort Commander and both of your positions are going away. You aren't being let go. You'll keep your seniority, but Clay, you'll be a senior service tech again, and Claudia, you can choose dispatch or CSR."

Clay felt like his gut was being ripped out. He'd worked so hard to get to service manager and he thought he was doing a pretty good job of it. Not just anyone could manage a bunch of service techs. In some ways, it was like herding cats, but Clay was good at it. Now he wished he'd gotten his contractor's license. If he had, no issues. He would start his own company. It was something he was going to do down the road. Unfortunately, he just ran out of road.

Clay listened to Will and Claudia review options in a fog. Claudia would take what they offered. She was a single mother and didn't have a choice. Clay, on the other hand, was childless and, according to the docs, he and his wife, Lynn, were unlikely to ever have one.

"What if I say no?" asked Clay. "What if I don't want to go back in a truck?"

Will leaned back and made an upside-down vee with his hands and pursed his lips on it. "I can get you six weeks," he said.

Six weeks, Clay thought. Well, if he couldn't find a service manager's job in six weeks he could always go to work for another company as a technician. It wouldn't be worse than what Riverrock was offering, and maybe he would come out ahead. "Done," he said.

***

Clay grabbed his things and went home. He'd have to tell Lynn, but it could wait. He wanted to be able to show progress in finding a new job before he told her he quit. Fortunately, she had a steady job as a teacher, so they had her income no matter what.

Clay made a mental list of the people he needed to call. He would start with Air Equipment Distribution. Before he could dial his phone, it chimed with a text. *Not now*, he thought. Word must already be spreading. But the text wasn't what he thought it would be...

> Incredible Opportunity — Become the chief of operations for a storied family business, whose owner is looking to step down. Must have a servant's heart, good management skills, practical technical aptitude, an ability to excel under pressure, and a tolerance for seasonal business variability. Excellent compensation package. Reply YES to inquire, NO to stop receiving texts.

Wow, thought Clay. *This is me.* It was from an 800 number, so he had no idea who sent it. He replied *yes* immediately. A second later, a new text appeared...

> We have an interview available at 11:00 a.m. at the Yuletide Inn and Conference Center. Reply YES to accept.

11:00 a.m.? That wasn't much time. It didn't matter. He would make it. He could almost envision getting out of the need to tell Lynn he quit his job and instead tell her he got a better one! He replied *yes* before realizing he had no idea where the Yuletide Inn was located. Clay knew the area like the back of his hand, but not this place. Almost as soon as he completed the thought, another text came in...

> Click for directions.

He clicked and KringleMaps, an app he didn't realize he had, popped open and gave him directions. It seemed strange. The directions led to a Highway 18 Tunnel and stopped. Where was he supposed to go when he got to the other side? He didn't care. This gave him a goal to pursue, so he started his truck and put it in drive. He wanted to be in motion.

***

When Clay arrived at the Highway 18 Tunnel north of town, the map hadn't changed. Oh well, he thought, I'll drive through and maybe it will kick in on the other side of the mountain.

Clay had driven through this tunnel dozens of times, but he never remembered the light show. It must have been something recently installed. Waves of pastel lights undulated around him. The tunnel was longer than he remembered.

Suddenly, Clay emerged. He looked around. There was snow on the ground. Snow? Must be a microclimate, stopped by the mountain. Up ahead he saw a sign directing him to the Yuletide Inn and Conference Center. Strange, he'd never seen the sign or the road before. Must be new.

Clay pulled up to the front of the inn. As soon as he got out, a black-and-brown Harley Davidson motorcycle screamed down the drive and slid sideways to a perfect stop. A portly old man in a leather jacket and biker boots jumped off and removed his helmet, revealing a *Duck Dynasty* beard and a head topped with a tied-off red bandana. "You must be Clay," he roared.

"Uh, yes, sir. I'm here for an interview."

"That you are, laddie. Come with me. We'll get started," said the man before stopping cold. "Oh, sorry. My name's... well, you can call me Chris." He extended a hand.

Clay shook it. He instantly liked the biker. He seemed naturally, well, *jovial*.

"Come on," said Chris. "Let's go inside."

When they walked into the inn Clay did a double take. It seemed way larger than he thought it would be. There was a huge stone fireplace with a roaring fire and in the corner was a large Christmas tree.

"Come, come with me into the library," said Chris. He turned and shouted, "Mary! Oh, Mary, would you bring us something hot to drink? The young man I was talking about is here."

Clay walked behind Chris and took a seat at a battleship-sized conference table that was covered with various antiques, from puzzles and small games to miscellaneous knickknacks. The walls were covered with old books, *very* old books. No sooner had he sat down than a woman bustled into the study with two cups and saucers.

"Here, love," she said as she placed one saucer before Chris. "I hope you like hot chocolate," she said, placing the other in front of Clay.

"Yes, ma'am. Thank you," said Clay. He sipped the chocolate. It was amazing. "Wow, this is terrific."

"Isn't it delicious?" observed Chris. "Mary makes the best hot chocolate in all of the world."

"Oh you," said Mary, clearly pleased. "Well, I'll leave you two to talk."

"Now," said Chris. "Let's talk a little business."

"Yes, sir," said Clay. "Um, what is the business?"

"That's rather complicated. Like heating and air conditioning, I'm in the service business."

"Hey, wait a sec. I never said I worked in HVAC."

"You didn't? You must have. Or else how would I have known?"

"I don't know..."

"Well, it's not important. Tell me what you think of running a service business."

"We respond to people's needs. We do our best to deliver comfort where people work and live. Or, well, I *used* to."

"Yes, I understand you left your employment."

"How could you know that?"

"Clearly you must have quit or you wouldn't be interviewing with me. Now, more about your philosophy of service."

Clay shifted in his seat. "Okay, the thing is that people need us when they need us and we've got to respond fast. But that's only part of it. We have to understand what they really need and try to help them understand our solutions."

"Oh?" asked Chris with a raised eyebrow. "How so?"

"A lot of the time we can fix a broken furnace or air conditioner, but that's not necessarily in the homeowner's best interests. We make the repair on an old system and, while it's working again, it's still an old system. They'll pay more in utilities than if they had a newer, more efficient system, face future expensive breakdowns, and still be confronted with the need to replace that old system in a year, two, or maybe three."

"Is that always the case?"

"No. Sometimes people just want it fixed as inexpensively as possible because they're planning on moving. Sometimes they just can't afford the expense."

"How do you know?"

"It's not easy. We ask questions. Sometimes they tell us. Sometimes we have to feel it out. And if it's something like affordability, we have to find a way to make it affordable with financing, for example."

"Interesting," said Chris. "Well, my business also requires you to perceive people's needs and wants. Moreover, you must desire, sincerely desire, to serve them."

"So, what is your business?"

"Tell me about how you manage your crew."

Clay laughed. "It's kind of a misnomer to say you manage service techs. You prepare them and point them. Really, you lead."

"How so?"

"You better be authentic. They'll sense it if you aren't. You can't ask people to do things they don't believe in or that conflict with their values. You try to direct them to places where they can win. These guys are really good, but a lot of them are insecure. They try to bluster their way through or act cynical when they are out of their comfort zone. Take performance pay."

"Yes?"

"It's new and some guys resisted it, even though they would make more money when they switched to performance pay and they would get more control over their jobs. So, I picked one guy who stood to do well under it and who was a vocal leader. I got him to try it as an experiment where he got paid by performance pay or straight time, whichever was higher. He ended up selling himself and, once he was sold, he sold everyone else."

"Interesting. So what do you do when there's a rush? I understand your business is somewhat seasonal."

"Somewhat? It's all seasonal. Will, the owner, tries to fight it, but we still see a rush during extreme weather."

"So what do you do?"

"You prepare. You balance out the peak season with the off-season. Make sure guys take off when the work slacks. But once the weather kicks in, it's all hands on deck."

"Our businesses are remarkably similar. We both have to lead groups who can be a challenge. We both serve others and have to perceive their needs and desires. We both face extreme seasonality, though mine is a tad worse than yours. And we both serve people in their homes."

"So what business are you in if you aren't in HVAC?" asked Clay.

"First, Clay, tell me what you want. I know you're a good soul, with a good heart, but what is your heart's desire? What do you want out of a job? Out of life?"

Clay rocked back. Hmm. What did he want? "I want to make a difference," he offered. "I want to do work that's important and that makes people happy. That's the great thing about HVAC. We leave people better than when we arrived. They're happy to see us. I don't mind the rush when it comes. It's an adrenaline rush. I don't think I would like it year-round, but seasonally? I thrive on it. But really, it's doing work that matters that's important."

Chris looked at him. "So do you want to know what the job's all about?"

"Of course."

"I think I need to show you. Can you ride a bike?"

"Bicycle or motorcycle?"

"A hog. Great, big hog."

"Let's go."

Chris led Clay outside. Where his Harley had been, there were now two of them. Chris told Clay to take the second. He jumped on, noting the model painted on the side. It read *Comet*.

Chris fired up his bike and told Clay to follow him. As they streaked down the road, it almost seemed like Chris's bike was running... with legs. Then, the bike lifted. Clay's eyes grew large. Chris was airborne and he was following. Clay nearly fell off when he looked down. He wasn't holding handlebars, but the horns of a massive deer.

Chris spiraled down to an Alpine village on his deer and Clay's mount followed. When they landed, they were surrounded by little people with pointed ears. Elves?

"Santa! Santa!" they chorused. "Is this him? Is this the new Santa?"

"Well," said Chris. "That's to be determined. Give him room. I'm going to give him a tour."

This isn't happening, Clay thought. *Elves? Flying reindeer? Big reindeer.*

Chris looked at him and pulled off his bandana. Freed from the confines of the scarf, with his white *Duck Dynasty* beard, Chris did look like Santa. He turned to Clay and said, "It's a lot to take in all at once."

Clay just gaped and nodded.

"Come on," said Chris. "Obviously, I'm not the first Santa. He lived in the third century and got his start in Turkey. Santas are granted long lives and typically serve more than a century but, eventually, even the longest-lived must step aside. I'm the 17th." Chris reached inside his leather jacket and pulled out a business card.

Kris Kringle XVII
Santa Claus
St. (unofficial) Nicholas

"If you accept the job you would become the 18th. Technically, you'd be our first Santa from the heating and air conditioning industry. I was a plumber. The Santa before me distributed coal to people to burn to keep warm, as did the Santa before him. I think that's where the idea of coal in the stocking came from."

"Now wait just a second..."

"I know, I know. You haven't accepted the job. But you will. I know these things. You know, 'I know when you've been sleeping; I know when you're awake,' and all of that. Every century or so, it's up to the current Santa to find an apprentice who, if things go as they should, will take over the family business. Follow me. Let's start in the workshop."

"You're... you're asking me to believe in Santa Claus? In a fairy tale?" sputtered Clay.

"Believe what you see before you."

When Clay looked again at Chris or Kris or whoever he was, the biker jacket had turned into a red, fur-lined coat. The motorcycle boots were simple black leather. He turned and walked through a storefront door on the village's main street. Clay saw dozens, no, hundreds of elves looking back at him. He scrambled after Kris.

The door opened onto a landing that overlooked a massive toy factory. The ceiling was 50 feet high and the floor was 50 feet deep, despite the store being one story tall. Elves were everywhere.

There were elves working on boxes over conveyor belts that reminded Clay of airport luggage scanners, only here brand new toys popped out, complete with their commercial packaging. It was all too much.

"Why me?" he finally asked, looking at Kris.

Kris smiled benignly. "You meet the requirements. I know you have a good heart. Remember, I KNOW these things. Yet that's not enough. You have a servant's heart. You understand how to serve others. You have the natural intuition to see into people's needs and desires that can be molded and developed with a little Christmas magic. You can lead and manage the barely manageable. Believe me, this will also take some development and magic. It's a stretch to call a colony of elves barely manageable."

The old man continued. "You also thrive on pressure. If you couldn't handle the seasonality of the heating and air conditioning business, you certainly couldn't handle Christmas. But you can. Now, I already knew all of these things, but I still needed to ask you. I like to check things twice."

Head already swimming, Clay asked, "If you're real, I mean *really* real, how is all of this possible?"

"Ah. Well, there is quite a bit of magic around. This is Christmas magic, which is some of the strongest. Christmas is a holy time when we celebrate the birth of Jesus, who is our greatest gift. We also remember how the Wise Men gave gifts to the baby Jesus. The birth of Christ was a magical time for the whole world and the magic continues to this day."

"And how do elves factor in?"

"The elves you see here are converts from the ancient gods to the true God. This is how they serve."

"Wait just a minute. Are you saying these are 'Christian elves?' They believe in Jesus?"

"Why is that hard to believe? Even demons believe in Jesus."

Clay scratched his head. He hadn't really thought of that.

Still, it was a lot to consider. A lot to take in. If Kris told him this, he would have written him off as a nutcase, but he *showed* him. Clay turned in a circle. He thought of Lynn. "What about my wife? I'm married."

Kris laughed. "Of course you are. It's a requirement. You met my wife, Mary. She's the 17th Mary Christmas. Lynn will be the 18th."

"I... I've got to talk with her."

"Of course you do. But she won't believe in this any more than you would without visiting. Take her to dinner tonight at the Inn."

***

When Clay returned from the tunnel in his truck that evening he was shocked to discover that, even though he had been gone for hours, almost no time had elapsed. He didn't know if he wanted to take over from Kris or not, but he had to admit the idea was intriguing.

When Clay took Lynn to the Inn, she seemed to immediately bond with Mary, like he had with Kris. Instead of riding Harleys, Kris suggested a sleigh ride. And what a ride it was, at least for Lynn.

As they stood in Santa's village, watching the elves running back and forth under a gentle snowfall, Clay asked Lynn, "What do you think?"

"I loved the little school with all the elvish children. I think we could be happy here. Did Mary tell you that one of the reasons we were picked was we're childless and both orphans?"

"No. I didn't even think about that."

"It's sad in a way. No one would really miss us, but if we come up here, well... Everyone would count on us every Christmas, especially on you. You know what bothers me the most?"

"What's that?"

"I don't want to change my name," Lynn said. "On the other hand, you've always liked helping people and I've always loved children and while you never say anything, I know we're both disappointed we can't have kids, but if we do this, all of the world's children would be ours in a way."

When the couple walked back to Santa's cottage, he opened the door to welcome them. "Well?"

"We're in," said Clay.

"I knew you'd be. I know things. You will, too."

Contractor Stories

How Service Contractors Bring a Little Christmas Magic on Every Service Call...

- They serve people in their homes.

- They have the hearts of servants.

- They must identify what people need and want.

- They must manage the barely manageable.

- They must work well under pressure.

- They must be comfortable with a seasonal business.

Soli Deo Gloria

Looking for a Speaker?

Matt Michel has been a featured speaker at meetings and conferences across the United States, Canada, Australia, and Europe. His motivational keynote addresses rally and uplift audiences while delivering lasting content and messages. Besides speaking on *Contractor Stories,* some of Matt's most popular and powerful messages include *Leadership Principles, Success Principles, Staying Positive in a Negative World,* and *The Entrepreneur's Story.*

For more information on using Matt as a speaker for your event, reach out to him directly.

His email is: MattMichel@Mail.com

His LinkedIn page is LinkedIn.com/in/mattmichel/

His phone is 214.995.8889.

About the Author

Called "The Contractor's Advocate" by *Contracting Business Magazine* and "The Contractor's North Star" by *The Air Conditioning Heating & Refrigeration NEWS*, Matt Michel is a serial entrepreneur and an internationally recognized and highly acclaimed motivational and informational speaker.

He is the founder, past Chairman, CEO, and president of Service Nation Inc., which operates the Service Roundtable (the world's largest business alliance for service contractors), the Service Nation Alliance best practices group, the Retail Contractor Coalition branding alliance, and the Service World Expo (the premier trade show and conference for residential-service contractors). Previously, he founded the Aire Serv franchise system.

Under Matt's leadership, Service Nation was named to the Texas A&M Aggie 100 six times, the Dallas 100, Fort Worth 50, and Inc. 5000, including multiple citations in the top 75 service companies.

Matt has received numerous professional awards and distinctions, including being the youngest person to be inducted into the Contracting Business Hall of Fame, a recipient of *The Air Conditioning Heating & Refrigeration NEWS* Legends of HVAC Award, the inaugural recipient of the NATE Golden Toolbox Award, and the Sigma Chi Fraternity's Significant Sig Award. *Contracting Business Magazine* named Matt one of the "22 most influential people in the history of the HVACR industry." *Contractor Maga-*

zine named him one of the "18 most influential people in the history of the plumbing/hydronics industries," and the *Air Conditioning NEWS* named him one of the "top five business advisors in the HVAC industry."

Personally, Matt has won four blue ribbons from the State Fair of Texas for salsa and several other cooking awards.

Today, Matt is a writer, speaker, and rancher. He and his wife, Pam, divide their time between their home in Shady Shores, Texas and their ranch outside of Gainesville, Texas. Matt can be reached by email at MattMichel@Mail.com or by phone at 214.995.8889.

www.ingramcontent.com/pod-product-compliance
Lightning Source LLC
Chambersburg PA
CBHW070201100426
42743CB00013B/3007